The Science of Sports

How Things In Sports Work

The Science of Sports

How Things In Sports Work

Sharon L. Blanding
and
John J. Monteleone

BARNES
&NOBLE
B O O K S
NEW YORK

Published by Barnes & Noble, Inc. by arrangement with Mountain Lion Inc.

A Mountain Lion Book

2003 Barnes & Noble Books

Text design by Lundquist Design, New York

ISBN 0 7607 3501 8

Printed and bound in the United States

03 04 05 06 07 08 TP 9 8 7 6 5 4 3 2 1

Contents

Contents continued

Chapter 1
Baseball

What makes a knuckleball flutter like a butterfly and a curveball curve?

"It's been going on in baseball for a hundred years. When pitchers make quality pitches, batters do not make good contact."

—Tony La Russa, Manager

Hitting a baseball—according to Baseball Hall of Fame player Ted Williams—is the most difficult feat accomplished in sports. Success certainly requires visual acumen and an exceptional sense of timing. A 90-mph fastball, moving at 132 feet per second (ft/sec), takes less than a half second to get to the plate. A batter has a quarter second to decide whether or not to swing, and another quarter second to get his bat positioned. A slow-moving knuckleball, traveling at 80 to 90 ft/sec, allows the batter seven-tenths of a second to respond—not much help against the unpredictable motion this ball presents.

Baseball is often called the game of failure, and with good reason. Most of the ball's "funny business" (curving or breaking) isn't discerned until the ball enters the last third of its trajectory—often too late for the batter to adjust his reactions. A phenomenal hitter may safely hit one out of three balls safely into fair territory, an abysmal average in most sports, though a mark of excellence in baseball.

The challenge a batter faces increases when the pitcher throws a knuckleball or curveball. Three distinct attributes make these pitches unique: the players' reactions, the physical phenomenon affecting the motion of the ball, and the special techniques required to throw the ball effectively.

The Knuckle Ball

Of all the pitches available to challenge a baseball player—fastballs, curveballs, sliders, split-fingers and screwballs, to name a few—none is so frustrating to hitters as the knuckleball. It's tough to throw (and control), tough to catch, and almost impossible to hit, but oh, what a delight to watch—if you're not at bat—as it dances, wobbles, dips, and flutters toward the plate **(see Figure 1–1)**.

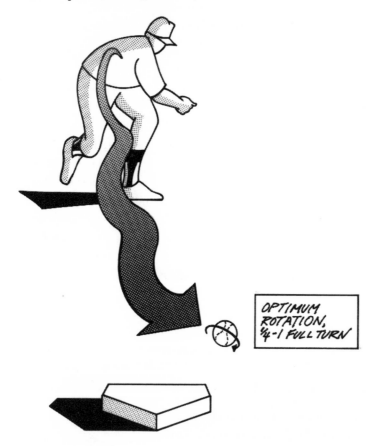

OPTIMUM ROTATION, ¼-1 FULL TURN

1-1   *Path of a Knuckleball. This unpredictable pitch dances, wobbles, dips, and flutters as it approaches the plate.*

Players' Reactions
Not many baseball players have the skill to be great knuckleball pitchers. For those players skillful at throwing the knuckleball, the years on the

mound are kind. The pitch is much easier on the arm than other throws, and some of the longest-playing major leaguers have been knuckleballers. Hoyt Wilhelm and Charlie Hough played until they were 49, Phil Niekro to 48 and Dutch Leonard to 44—real old-timers in this field.

Niekro believes the dearth of knuckleballers is the result of young baseball players having too many distractions—parties, music, computers, movies—and not enough practice. "You simply cannot take up the sport of baseball and become good at it if you only work out once or twice a week. You have to work hard at it six and seven days a week, and several hours each day." He and his father threw the knuckleball for hours at a time, trying to minimize the spin and seeing who could make the ball do more things.

Practice doesn't help catchers, however, who genuinely earn their salaries when knuckleballers are on the mound. Bob Uecker, while with the Atlanta Braves, said he needed four days' rest between games that "Knucksie" Niekro pitched just "to get over chasing that knuckleball all over the place." He's also famous for the statement, "The best way to catch a knuckleball is to wait for it to stop rolling and pick it up." John Blanchard, who was also on Niekro's team, agrees: "There are two different schools of thought on how to catch a knuckle ball—and neither works." When a known knuckleballer is pitching, catchers don the largest permitted mitt in an attempt to decrease the number of passed balls.

Physical Phenomenon

What makes a knuckleball so special? Primarily its unpredictability—not even the pitcher is sure where the ball will end up when it completes the 60½-foot journey to the plate. Two major conditions contribute to the flutter manifested by a knuckleball: a lack of spin and a disruption of air flow caused by the stitches on the cover.

Regardless of the type of pitch, as a ball sails through the air, two things happen: the direction of air in front of the ball changes to accommodate the ball's slicing through it, and the air closest to the ball slows down because of friction, also known as drag. Friction results because air has a measurable density (about two pounds per cubic yard), which the ball must force its way through. This friction can substantially

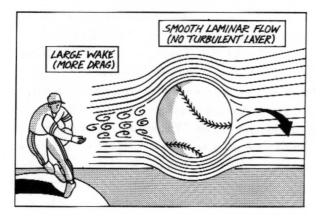

1-2 *Knuckleball Traveling Below Critical Speed. With a smooth laminar flow of air surrounding the ball and no turbulent layer, a large wake forms behind he ball, causing it to slow and drop.*

1-2b *Knuckleball Traveling Above Critical Speed. The turbulent air surrounding the ball provides little drag, and so the ball travels straight longer.*

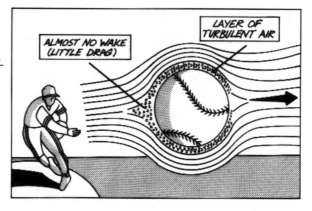

reduce the speed of flight. At slow speeds, the air in front of the ball smoothly "parts" to allow the ball through (laminar flow). The air layer next to the ball is easily torn away and forms a large wake behind the ball (drag) **(see Figure 1–2).** When the ball is moving at high speeds, however, smooth flow is no longer possible. The air next to the ball becomes erratic (turbulent), and is hugged against the ball; little wake or drag occurs to slow the ball down **(see Figure 1–2b).**

As a ball spins, half of its surface area is with the flow of air; the other half is against it. This condition creates differences in air pressure, which in turn cause a deviation, or curve, in the flight path. The ball always deviates in the direction of its spin; a phenomenon known as the

Magnus effect. However, a knuckleball barely spins, so it isn't the Magnus effect that causes its "deviation."

Is the deviation caused by the ball's slow motion? Knuckleballs travel about 50 mph (although Phil Niekro threw them at 65 mph), considerably less than most pro fastballs, which range from 85 mph to 99 mph. Since the ball is moving so slowly, and generally carries minimum spin, it seems logical that air currents would more readily affect its flight pattern. However, experiments show that it is the air flow immediately next to the ball that causes the motion, not the errant breezes blowing across the diamond.

The mysterious flutter of the knuckleball has always fascinated scientifically inclined baseball fans. A team of engineers under Joel W. Hollenberg, professor of mechanical engineering at the Cooper Union for the Advancement of Science and Art in New York, spent six years, beginning in 1982, looking for an answer. His team confirmed earlier findings that the odd behavior of the ball does indeed arise from its very slow spin and the aerodynamic properties of the raised stitches. Using wind tunnels, they found that the drag encountered by the baseball varied with its velocity and the orientation of its stitches. By gluing strips of silk around the ball, the team confirmed that drag tends to be higher when the flow of air around the ball is smooth (laminar), and lower when the flow is rough (turbulent). Hollenberg believes that a ball undergoes an actual change of direction as it passes from turbulent to laminar flow.

This finding reinforced what earlier physicists had said all along, particularly Robert Watts, one of our most active "baseball scientists." Watts, a mechanical engineer at Tulane University, found that the optimum spin for a lively knuckleball is between one-quarter and one full revolution between the mound and home plate. By using a wind tunnel that generated air flows between 40 and 70 ft/sec, he found that as a ball slowly spins, lateral forces can vary from 0.1 to 0.18 pounds—the latter occurring when the ball is at 52 and 310 degrees from its initial starting point (0 degrees). At these angles, turbulent air flow caused the lateral forces to alternate from left to right at 0.5-second intervals. Now, isn't it easy to see how such forces could make a knuckleball flutter! Watts and Hollenberg agree that the ball's dip and hop occur when the air changes from turbulent to laminar flow.

Such information begs to be computerized, so Hollenberg and his team combined their data with that from other institutions to produce a computer modeling program on knuckleball throws. The user enters the position, spin, direction, and velocity of the ball at the moment of release, and the program predicts how the ball will react. It also calculates the effects of wind, temperature, barometric pressure, and humidity. According to this model, knuckleballs should become less lively as temperatures rise. Hollenberg may be right about that, but on a warm day, if the batter does manage to make contact with the ball, a homer is more likely to result.

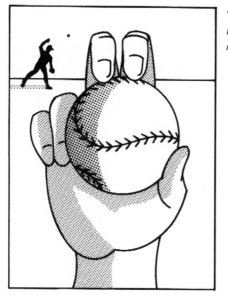

1-3 *Grip for a Knuckleball. The ball is held on the seams with the fingertips, not with the knuckles, which protrude.*

Technique

To fly like a butterfly, a knuckleball must be thrown in a very precise manner. To minimize spin, pitchers grip the ball tightly with their fingertips (this causes the knuckles to protrude, hence the name) and the ball is lobbed, or pushed, more than it is thrown **(see Figure 1-3).** Niekro dug his forefinger and middle finger into the stitched seams. The wrist is kept locked. Most coaches recommend that a player grasp the ball in the same location, relative to the stitches, each time it is thrown to ensure consistency.

If a pitcher hasn't mastered the skill of knuckleball throwing, there are other ways to induce similar effects. Although it has been illegal since 1920, players still "doctor" the ball. There is a saying that the best way to get the better of temptation is just to yield to it, and apparently many pitchers do: some estimates place one-third to one-half of all major league pitches in this "doctored" category. It's easy enough to do. If one side of the ball is rougher than the other, drag will be affected. A saliva-laden spitball can act just like a fast, wet knuckleball. Although the ball will still spin, extra air resistance makes its motion erratic and hard for a batter to hit.

Some players will go to any length to make one side of the ball smoother—for example, with spit or hair grease—or to make one side rougher, by scuffing, sanding, or fingernail cuts. Lefty Grove, when asked if he threw a spitball, replied, "Not intentionally, but I sweat easy." Seattle Mariner Gaylord Perry was suspended for ten days because he doctored the ball. He freely admitted to applying such foreign substances as saliva, Vaseline, K-Y Jelly, and fishing line wax. One batter could still hit him, however; Perry unabashedly says of Rod Carew, "He's the only player in baseball who consistently hits my grease. He sees the ball so well, I guess he can pick out the dry side."

Batters with less visual acuity can find solace in the fact that what's good for the goose is good for the gander. A pitcher scuffing up a ball may unwittingly increase the odds for a homer—if the batter manages to hit the ball. The lack of drag can work both ways.

A player can technically remain legal and roughen up the stitches by squeezing the ball or scraping it with his fingernails. Umpires frequently inspect the balls for this reason and reject any that show signs of hanky-panky.

Will knowing the physics behind a knuckleball's erratic flight help a batter to hit it? Probably not. Orel Hershiser, a Cy Young winner with the Dodgers, says: "Batters don't change. That's why knuckleball pitchers, screwball pitchers, and specialty-pitch pitchers do so well, because batters won't change that one day and risk ruining the other four."

1-4 *Path of a Curveball. Continuous curve or sudden break? The curveball actually moves laterally and down in a continuous curve.*

The Curveball

The curveball, like the knuckleball, can credit the stitches on the ball for its swinging motion to the plate. Dodger Carl Furillo, in a moment of frustration, said it well: "Carrots might be good for my eyes, but they won't straighten out the curveball."

Players' Reactions

High-tech equipment and experiments have confirmed what every ballplayer has always known: the ball does curve. What physicists and players still disagree on is the matter of the "breaking ball." Players swear that a skillfully pitched curveball flies straight and then suddenly "breaks," normally too late for the batter to do anything about it. Physicists maintain that such a move is impossible under Newtonian physics, and that the ball's motion follows a continuous curve **(see Figure 1–4)**. Just go up against one of Pedro Martinez's explosive curveballs, the ballplayers argue, and that will hurry you back to your blackboards. This dispute has been going on since the game began.

Einstein can help a little here with his discovery that motion is relative. The location of the observer in relation to the object moving will define what he or she perceives. In other words, two people seeing the same motion will perceive it differently.

Visualize a train running on a circular track. If you are standing at the radius point and far enough away from the track, you will see the train maintaining a constant speed and direction. But if you move to the edge of the track, you will observe the train apparently coming straight toward you and then suddenly breaking left or right, depending upon your location on the curve. The speed and direction of the train haven't changed—but your perception of them has. This optical illusion is even more intense for a batter because as he steps towards the pitcher (and oncoming ball) his motion adds further distortion.

Physical Phenomenon

Baseballs curve from the same forces that enable an airplane to fly. A spinning ball causes pressure variances that create "lift," which can induce an upward, downward, or sideways motion. The magnitude of the resulting curve depends more on spin than speed. A faster rotation produces a larger curve. This force, along with gravity and drag, is present from the moment the ball leaves the pitcher's hand **(see Figure 1–5)**. The reason why a spectator can't see the curve in the beginning of the flight is that the eye is too slow to follow the actual path of the curve. Nonetheless, it is there. So, in this regard, the physicists are right.

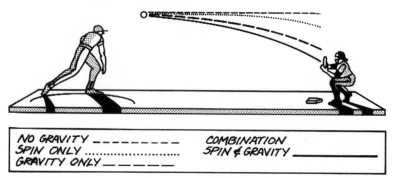

NO GRAVITY _ _ _ _ _ _ _ _ _ _   COMBINATION
SPIN ONLY ....   SPIN & GRAVITY _____
GRAVITY ONLY _ _ _ _ _ _

1-5 *Spin + Gravity = Curveball. When a ball is thrown with horizontal topspin it is pushed down. When the curving force is in the same direction as gravity (what is known as a 12-to-6 curveball), a curveball falls faster and farther (more than 1 foot over 60 feet, 6 inches) than any other pitch, as shown by the solid line.*

On the other hand, the research done by Watts and Hollenberg shows that when a ball passes through a critical speed zone and turbulent air flow changes to laminar, actual change of direction can occur. This phenomenon may explain the "break" the batters see and that they swear is not an optical illusion.

In any event, a good pitcher taking advantage of these aerodynamic principles can get a ball to seriously deviate from a straight line. Lyman J. Briggs, former director of the National Bureau of Standards, found that a ball rotating eighteen times on its way to the plate can curve as much as 17½ inches. (A 98-mph Randy Johnson fastball can rotate up to 40 times.) Likewise, a ball thrown with enough speed and backspin can actually overpower the forces of gravity and drag, making it appear to rise. However, most pitchers prefer to make the ball curve downward because this makes it harder for a batter to calculate where to swing. A downward curve will occur if the seams of the ball are perpendicular to the direction in which the ball is thrown.

Technique

A curveball is thrown with a forceful, downward spin and crisp snap of the wrist. Rotation is more important than speed. The hand lies against one side of the ball, with the fingers on top, often with one of the fingers alongside a seam **(see Figure 1–6)**. Thumb location varies with the pitcher. Koufax had a bum index finger but by applying pressure with his middle finger alone was able to throw curveballs with incredible force and break. Dutchman Bert Blyleven credits his extraordinary curveball to very long fingers, "developed from sticking my fingers into dikes."

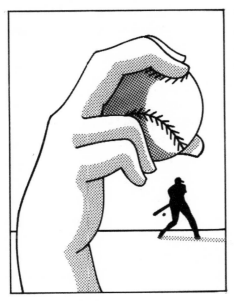

1-6 *Grip for a Curveball. For a curveball, the hand lies against one side of the ball with the fingers on top.*

Tom Seaver grasped his curveball like his fastball—the index and middle fingers placed across the seams where they are farthest apart. However, on his curveball he covered some of the surface with finger pressure. He advises throwing a curve from top to bottom, not from back to front. That is, a right-handed pitcher should release the ball from behind his right ear and follow through to the outside of his left leg. Seaver's three absolutes for a successful curveball are: (1) keep your fingers on top of the ball, (2) keep your elbows above your shoulder, and (3) get it out, get it up; that is, get the ball out of your glove and into throwing position as soon as you can.

The Ideal Characteristics of a Wooden Baseball Bat

A little more than a hundred years ago, hemlock was the wood of choice for bat construction. White ash, usually from New York or Pennsylvania, is now favored, although maple recently has made inroads with some major league players. As ash becomes scarcer, however, manufacturers are experimenting with other materials, notably graphite.

Most amateur leagues and college teams use aluminum bats. Rookies entering professional baseball, where wood is used exclusively, encounter problems because wooden bats have a much smaller sweet spot than metal bats. Tests show that balls slugged by aluminum go 10 percent farther than those hit by wood—enough to change the record books. This isn't the only reason why the majors are unlikely to switch to this material soon. Ken Griffey, Jr. says it best: "You'd better move the mound back ten feet and give everybody life insurance, because somebody will get killed." Because increased speed at which the ball leaves a metal bat, most players agree that metal bats pose a serious threat to pitchers and first and third basemen.

Wooden bats today generally weigh between 32 and 34 ounces; most metal bats weight 32 ounces or less. Hack Miller supposedly used the heaviest bat on record. He played his one and only professional season in 1923 with a 65-ounce log, and must have worn himself out. Reds outfielder Edd Roush (1913–1931) was next in line at 48 ounces. Wee Willie Keeler, Billy Goodman, Joe Morgan, and Tony Gwynn favored light bats—30 ounces. Keeler's was also the shortest (30½ inches), but he himself only measured 5' 4½". Hall of Famer Al Simmons had the longest bat at 38 inches. Although the rule book states that a bat can be 42 inches long, there is no record of anyone having used that length. The rules also state that a bat should be a "smooth, rounded stick" (no paddles) and no more that 2¾ inches in diameter at its thickest part. There are no restrictions on weight.

It's not uncommon for players to develop compulsive relationships with their bats. Ted Williams supposedly sent an entire shipment back because the handles were off by 0.005 inch. Orlando Cepeda was so positive that each bat was good for only a limited number of hits that he would discard one after reaching that number. At the other extreme, Joe Sewell used one bat for fourteen seasons, hammering out 2,226 hits. Shoeless Joe Jackson sent his bats to South Carolina for the winter, believing they should stay warm.

There's more to a successful hit than just connecting ash with cowhide. Complex mechanical forces come into play, some understood, some not. As a hitter brings the bat toward the contact point, his hands exert a backward rotational effect, or torque, on the bat handle. Torque defines how effective a force is in producing rotation. It is computed by multiplying the length of a "lever" by the amount of force applied at the end of the lever. If a person uses a 2-foot-long crowbar as a lever, for example, and applies 100 pounds of force, he generates 200 foot-pounds of torque. Hence, the amount of torque generated is directly proportional to the distance between the force and the pivot point, and on the strength of the force. Because the head of the bat is heavier than the handle, and is farther away from the pivot point (the batter's hand), it exerts more torque. Torque adds momentum and power to the bat's motion, and on a successful hit, transfers to the ball. The exact amount of torque a player generates varies, depending on the batter's weight and the size of his hands, and on the weight of the bat.

By gripping the bat tightly, the batter increases the effective mass of the bat by making it an extension of his own body (increasing the length of the "lever"). As much as 1,500 pounds of force can thereby be generated. The sweet spot on a bat (about four inches down from the end of the barrel) is the best contact point.

The speed of the bat is more important than its weight in determining how far a ball will travel. Al Campanis, former Dodger executive, puts it succinctly: "It has been proven that energy or force is equal to mass times velocity squared. In applying this formula to batting, the significant factor is velocity, since it is squared." For each mile an hour increase in bat speed, a batter should be able to get five extra feet out of the drive.

Hence, a smaller barrel increases homers because it moves faster. It also increases strikeouts—more balls are completely missed. But, no pain, no gain. As Mike Schmidt said, after winning his third consecutive home run title in 1976: "A guy who strikes out as much as I do had better lead in something." A thinner handle can also reduce the weight of a bat, but the possibility of breakage is substantially increased.

Calculations relating mass and velocity show that the ideal bat would weight 20 ounces. However, because regulations governing professional baseball require a bat to be solid wood, a bat of this weight would be either too short or too thin to be effective.

To make their bats stronger or lighter, players indulge in a number of legal and illegal activities. Boning is legal but of questionable efficacy. Some players swear that rubbing the sweet spot of the bat with a bone, pop bottle, or railroad spike will close the pores and strengthen the wood. "Yeah, I used to bone 'em," says former slugger Frank Howard. "I'd spend two hours boning 'em and rubbing 'em and then the first time up, I'd hit one off the end or on the handle and break the damn bat."

Corking a bat is an illegal attempt to reduce its weight. A hole, drilled 8 inches into the head of a bat and filled with cork, can reduce the weight by 1.5 ounces, about the amount needed to increase the bat speed by one mph. Billy Hatcher, of the Astros, was caught in this shenanigan when his bat shattered and sprayed cork all over the field. An accepted legal procedure to reduce the weight of a bat involves carving a dent in the head of the bat one inch deep and two inches wide, which reduces the weight by approximately one-half ounce.

Warm Winds and Home Run Blasts

"No home run today—blame it on the weather!"

The theory that warm weather increases the number of home runs is sometimes called, appropriately, the Chernobyl Theory. Heat can undoubtedly turn a two- or three-bagger into a homer. Norman A. Matson, a Seattle weatherman, has studied the subject in depth, in conjunction with Sir Graham Sutton, a noted British meteorologist.

Matson used the following example to show author and columnist Walter Rue the principles behind the theory. In both scenarios the velocity of the ball immediately after impact is 147 feet per second, and it leaves the bat at a 30-degree angle to the horizontal plane. The games are at the Kingdome in Seattle (former home of the Mariners), which is, for practical purposes, at sea level.

In the first scenario, the day is a warm 95° F, resulting in an air density of 0.071 pounds per cubic foot. After one second of flight time, the velocity of the ball decreases to 120 feet per second (ft/sec). After four seconds the ball is going 78 ft/sec. It completes its arc and hits the bleachers 360 feet from the plate—a homer **(see Figure 1–7)**.

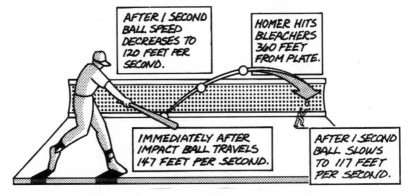

1-7   *Scenario No. 1. Daytime, 95° F, air density 0.071 pounds per cubic foot. Because of the decreased air density, a long fly ball struck in hot or humid weather, or at a high altitude, is more likely to be a home run.*

The second scenario is a night game and the air has chilled to 50° F. Air density is thick—0.077 pounds per cubic foot. The ball starts out at the same velocity, 147 ft/sec. At touchdown the ball is only 345 feet from the plate, 15 feet short of the daytime slug. In a game of inches, that's a significant difference **(see Figure 1–8)**.

Clearly, temperature can dramatically affect the outcome of a game. Air density, and subsequent homers, can also be affected by changes in humidity and atmospheric pressure.

Moist air is lighter than dry air, although the skin may inaccurately perceive moist air as "heavier." When the weather is dry, barometric pressure rises (more pressure); when stormy, the barometer falls (lower pressure). As air pressure increases and the air gets drier, it contracts and allows more air molecules per cubic foot; hence, the air is denser.

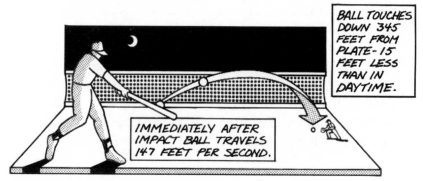

1-8   *Scenario No. 2. Nightime, 50° F, air density 0.077 pounds per cubic foot. The cold air of some night games means thicker air density, which causes balls to move more slowly and fall to the ground sooner.*

Altitude makes a big difference in air density. Atmospheric pressure results from the aggregate weight of the air above an object. Therefore, the higher an object, the less "weight" bearing down on it. The density of air in Denver (at 5,200 feet) would be 0.0597 pound per cubic foot at 95° F and 0.0650 at 50° F. Hence, at either of these temperatures the ball will travel farther in Denver than it does in Seattle (even on a hot day).

Anatomy of a Baseball

Is there more bounce to the ounce in some baseballs? That's the question of the day when homers see a banner year, as happened in 1987. That year saw 4,458 major league homers, as compared to 3,813 in 1986 and a mere 3,085 in 1989.

Called everything from live rabbits, juiced balls, live balls, to bunny baseballs and rabid rabbits (but not, as yet, juiced rabbits), this major component of a ball game gets most of the credit when an outlandish number of homers are made.

Impossible, says a spokesman for Rawlings Sporting Goods Company, the company that has since 1977 produced about 600,000 balls a year for the major leagues. The ball hasn't changed in composition since 1931, when a cork center was replaced with a cushioned cork center.

The remaining inner components have stayed the same: the small cork sphere is covered with a thick layer of black rubber, then a thinner layer of red rubber, then four layers of wound yarn (about 300 yards). Cowhide is glued on the outside (horsehide was used until 1973), and the ball is hand-stitched (216 stitches if you count each herringbone as two stitches, which is technically correct, or 108 if counted singly). By regulation the ball must weigh between 5 and 5¼ ounces and have a 9 to 9¼-inch circumference.

"Bounce," or how far a ball will go, is determined by the coefficient of restitution (COR), which is the ratio of the ball's velocity after a collision to its velocity before a collision. For major league baseballs, this ratio must be between 0.514 and 0.578, plus or minus 3.2 percent, which means that the rebound speed must be 51.4 percent to 57.8 percent of the original speed, plus or minus 3.2 percent. (By comparison, a tennis ball has a COR of 0.67 and a basketball 0.76.)

The homer explosion in 1987 caused such a hullabaloo that *USA Today* and league offices commissioned a scientific test from Haller Testing Laboratories of Plainfield, New Jersey. Tests were done on 116 baseballs collected from all twenty-six teams. In a separate test, the leagues requested the Science and Aeronautics Department of the University of Missouri to compare 1985 and 1987 balls. The conclusion: the balls of 1987 were not livelier.

If the ball can't be given credit, what can? Players and fans have many theories, including the following:

- Livelier players (less drinking, smoking, and womanizing)
- Stronger players (better fed; more exercise)
- Playing Nintendo has given the batters quicker hand-eye coordination
- Domed stadiums
- New ball parks, designed for producing more long hits
- The happy Haitian theory (when Haiti dictator Baby Doc Duvalier was overthrown, the Haitians—who make the balls for Rawlings— were so happy that they wound the balls tighter and/or sewed the seams tighter)
- Lively imaginations
- The weather

Unfortunately, such theories leave unexplained why 1989—when 3,089 homers were recorded—was such a bad year, unless, of course, the trend suggested in the first theory (livelier players) is reversing. Attitudes about carousing certainly change through the years. Casey Stengel, a renowned advocate of bending the elbow for activities other than pitching, once said, "We're in such a slump that even the ones that are drinkin' aren't hittin'." A new manager, Tony La Russa, says half of his players do not drink at all.

Whatever the reason behind the hits, extraordinary things happen to a baseball when it undergoes a collision with the bat. Physicist Robert Adair, former chairman of the physics department at Yale University and appointed in 1987 as the National League's designated physicist, explains:

> A baseball hitting a bat gets severely compressed. It may be flattened to about half its original size. As it is leaving the bat, however, it instantly springs back to shape. The energy generated by this adds speed to the ball. If the pitch comes in at ninety miles and hour, the hit will go back out at about a hundred and ten. Assuming it's someone like [Don] Mattingly swinging the bat, the next place you'll see the ball will usually be the upper deck.

And that's the way the ball bounces.

Chapter 2

Basketball

The Perfect Swish

"Swish! I love making that sound. When you shoot the basketball and it goes swish as it slips through the net, that's the sweetest sound of all."

— *Earvin "Magic" Johnson*

What makes a basketball go swish? No one knows better than Peter J. Brancazio. A physicist from City University of New York, Brancazio in 1981 published equations that tell the best angle, speed, and force a shot should have to ensure a score. He admits that in part he was motivated because of his own frustration as a ballplayer: he was short (5'9"), couldn't jump more than 8 inches off the floor, and was "old." Nonetheless, his love of the sport inspired him to use a computer to determine that:

- A ball spinning backward loses more energy when it hits an object— such as the rim of a basket, the backboard, or the floor—than does one without spin. The greater the amount of backspin, the greater the energy lost on impact. Consequently, such a ball will tend to drop into the basket rather than wildly bounce off the backboard
- The odds of scoring increase as the height of the launch point increases.
- For any specific distance and launching height, there exists an optimum launch angle. This favorable angle will also require the least launch speed, an advantage according to Brancazio because "the less force you put on it, the easier it is to get the shot off."

When a ball carrying no spin hits a surface, its forward motion changes into angular momentum, or forward spin. If the ball is traveling with a spin in the same direction as its motion (forward spin), spin decreases on impact but rebound speed increases. Backspin, however, decreases both spin and speed, thus encouraging the ball to fall into the basket. Backspin on a ball is generated by rolling the ball off the fingertips with a snap of the wrist **(see Figure 2-1)**.

2-1 *No Spin (Hard Rebound) Versus Backspin (Soft, Short Rebound).*
When a ball with no spin hits the backboard, its forward motion changes into angular momentum, or forward spin (top). A ball with backspin loses energy when it hits the backboard, encouraging it to drop into the basket (bottom).

Sidespin is used in other sports, such as golf and tennis, to put "slice" on the ball. This tactic isn't used in shooting a basketball, however, because, if the ball were to hit the backboard, sidespin would make it spin away from the basket. It is used, however, sometimes on a bounce pass intended to go past a defender and then veer toward the player being passed to.

Besides height, both the speed and force of the ball determine whether a shot succeeds. The "softness" of a shot (that is, the minimum speed required to get the ball to the basket) decreases with the distance to the basket. A perfect shot occurs when an ideal is reached between the angle and speed, or what Brancazio calls the minimum-force launch angle. His studies of the best shooters show that they intuitively shoot at this angle, which is approximately 45 degrees (between the floor and a line perpendicular to it) plus half the angle to the basket.

Table 2-1 shows the optimum launch angles, minimum launch speeds, and average forces calculated by Brancazio for a ball released eight feet above the floor.

Table 2-1

Effects of Distance to Basket on Launch Angle, Speed, and Force

DISTANCE TO BASKET (FEET)	MINIMUM LAUNCH ANGLE (DEGREES)	BEST LAUNCH ANGLE (DEGREES)	MINIMUM LAUNCH SPEED (FT/SEC)	AVERAGE LAUNCH FORCE (POUNDS)	MAXIMUM HEIGHT ABOVE RIM (FEET)
10	45.6	50.7	19.8	3.9	1.6
15	41.6	48.8	23.5	5.5	2.9
20	39.4	47.9	26.7	7.1	4.1
25	38.0	47.3	29.5	8.7	5.3

Used by permission from the American Association of Physics Teachers and Peter J. Brancazio

If a player is within ten feet of the basket, he will probably try a bank shot off the backboard, rather than an arched shot. These shots must be "soft," or the bounce will be overpowered.

The jumpshot, one of the most popular shots in the game, is often shot with a flat trajectory, partly because players tend to shoot at the same angle, regardless of the distance they are from the basket. However, as Brancazio shows, the closer a player is to the basket, the higher the angle that should be put on the shot. Brancazio took his theories to the court to prove them. Prior to his study, he normally used flat trajectories, "with consistently mediocre shots." He found that after only a few weeks of practicing with a higher launch angle, a "significant and very satisfying improvement in shooting accuracy" resulted.

On free throw shots, is the underhand or overhand technique better? Brancazio has concluded that underhand is better, because the shot is naturally thrown with a greater amount of backspin. Few players throw this way, however, which is surprising, because about 25 percent of all games are won by the success of free throw shots.

In general, most players claim that practicing an underhand shot for free throws conflicts with their overhand field goal shots. To mix the two might tamper with their "natural shooting ability." Of course, an underhand field-goal shot is easily blocked; hence, it is rarely used during play.

In past years, underhand shots prevailed for free throws. In fact, three studies done in the fifties and early sixties indicate that a larger percentage of the successful free throws were thrown underhand.

Rich Barry was the last of the great underhand free throw shooters. Since 1980, he has held the NBA record for the highest career free-throw percentage (.900). He wasn't bad with his overhand shots either.

However a shot is thrown, a higher arch increases the odds of its scoring. Because a ball 9.7 inches across has to enter an 18-inch-wide hoop, a higher arch effectively opens the "window" of the basket; that is, the area through which the ball can easily travel.

It seems apparent that a tall player should have an easier time making accurate shots, and Brancazio has shown mathematically that this is indeed the case. He concludes "given equal shooting abilities, a taller player has an advantage over a shorter one at any distance from the basket in that the taller player has a greater margin for error" **(see Figure 2–2)**. However, he adds, "fortunately for the shorter players, most taller players tend to develop their rebounding and under-the-basket play at the expense of their longer-distance shooting skills."

The eighties definitely saw a general increase in the height of players playing in the NBA. Wilt Chamberlain at 7'1" was the first of the great mobile seven footers, followed by Kareem Abdul-Jabbar at 7'2". Tom Burleson, Mark Eaton and Ralph Sampson all were 7'4", but had less well-developed skills.

Manute Bol, at 7'7", is the tallest player in NBA history. Suleiman Ali Nashnush, who at 8'0" played for the Libyan team in 1962, is reputed to be the tallest player of all time. Dazzling heights from which to throw a ball—or go for a jump ball. Under these conditions, a player's launch point can easily be higher than the 10-foot-high basket rim.

When very tall players first started entering the game, they had a reputation for being uncoordinated and slow. Things changed as athletes in all sports started to receive specialized training. Moreover, as the

2-2 *Higher Arch Varies with Three Players. With a greater margin for error, taller players have the advantage at any distance from the basket. The ball's angle of approach permits more off-center shots to fall through and score.*

"crop" of athletes who were both tall and naturally gifted expanded, the slower and less coordinated simply didn't advance to the pros. George Mikan, at 6'10", was the first outstanding "tall man" of the court, and he helped the Lakers win six NBA titles in his first seven years with the club. About the time Mikan retired, the 6'9" Bill Russell joined the Boston Celtics, and his remarkable rebounding and jumping skills left little doubt that "tall" could most definitely be an asset in basketball.

Tallness by itself doesn't guarantee a player success in shooting, nor that the shooter can effectively throw both field goal and free throw shots. For example, Wilt Chamberlain's strong inside offense allowed him to set many NBA records, which endure to this day. Yet his average at the free throw line was a paltry .511. Brancazio's analysis of the problem: "He was throwing line drives. He simply was not arching his shots enough."

About six years after Chamberlain retired, during the 1979–1980 season, the NBA initiated the three-point scoring rule, where a successful shot made from 23 feet 9 inches out and beyond scored 3 points instead of 2. This rule certainly has changed the complexion of the game, and some fans bemoan the fact that it has turned a game of skillful passing and teamwork into a "run'n'gun" game. Indeed, in 1980 NBA teams attempted three-pointers only 4.9 times a game, with a 24.5 percent success rate. Ten years later, with the advent of the long bomb specialist, this average had increased to 13.1 times a game, with a 32.3 percent success rate.

Dunk shots, where players shove the ball down through the ring with one or both hands, are among the most spectacular shots seen on the court. Some of the best "dunkers" are short, at least by current standards. Spud Webb, who beat seven challengers in a dunk contest at the 1986 All-Star game, is only 5'7". When Magic Johnson said "basketball isn't ballet, but it's close," he probably had dunk shots in mind. Leaps four feet off the ground are not uncommon. Look out, Mikhail Baryshnikov.

One aspect of the perfect swish not shown by Brancazio's charts is the millisecond reactions necessary for a human being to sight the basket, set up for, and then execute the shot.

First, a player often sees the ball only out of his peripheral vision, and must react quickly to it. Then, three separate parts of the brain are responsible for computing the angular distances between the line of sight and the moving ball, and these "computations" are compared and recalculated millisecond by millisecond. Depth perception keeps the ball in focus. Two eyes allow a person's brain to perceive stereoscopic vision patterns, which it then compares with past and present pattern as the ball moves closer and recedes. The brain makes these comparisons and calculations much faster than any computer yet designed.

Computers also lack our special ability to visualize events, a so-called "right-brain" activity. For a right-handed person, it is the left side of the brain that thinks and analyzes; the right side is responsible for "nonthinking" and visualization activities, including those that involve spatial relationships. Studies have shown that in most sports activities the left side of the brain initially sizes up the situation; then, as the athlete concentrates on and does the task at hand, the right side takes over. When we perform repetitive-type activities without thinking, we are "going with the flow" and using the right, nonthinking side of our brains. Errors ensue when we shift from automatic drive to thinking about the job at hand.

Even if a player has trained himself to "keep his cool," it is still difficult to maintain control and concentration at the end of a close-scoring game. Tensions run high and each player feels especially responsible for doing everything right—and can consequently think too hard. Control pays, however, and can generate great moments.

With only 14 seconds remaining in the 1989 playoff game between the Detroit Pistons and the L.A. Lakers, the Pistons held a lead of 102–99 and were fairly secure that the game was bagged. But within that short period Piston Bill Laimbeer fouled Kareem Abdul-Jabbar twice. At the foul line, pressure mounted, on fans, the TV audience, and on the shooter.

Kareem bounced the ball a few times and then . . . swish. Again . . . swish. Four times in all, and the Lakers won, 103–102. Says Kareem: "All my years of experience, all the times when I'd been able to stay detached and dispassionate, really served me well at that one moment. And it is actually easier sometimes to have all that pressure, because it can make you concentrate, and when you concentrate you can do extraordinary things." Unquestionably, Kareem was using the right side of his brain.

Sports psychologists have successfully used a technique called visuo-motor behavior rehearsal (VMBR) to improve athletes' skills. Using this technique, an athlete tenses his or her muscles, then relaxes and imagines the entire task he wants to improve. The scenario is repeated many times, and because there is no fear of failure, tension and other emotional barriers are eliminated. This "rehearsal" pays off later when the activity is actually done.

Richard Suinn, a Colorado State University psychologist, has shown what occurs physically when an athlete undergoes VMBR. He connected electromyograph (EMG) leads to an alpine skier's legs and had him go through the VMBR process. The skier visualized himself careening down an imaginary race course. Although his legs appeared to be relaxed, the EMG tape showed that electrical activity in the muscles mirrored each bump and turn on the course. In almost every sense, the skier was experiencing, and therefore practicing, the activity.

Henry Fensterheim, a psychologist at Cornell University, applied Suinn's studies to basketball. Comparing eight teams that used VMBR during the second half of the season, he found that "with VMBR the overall performance improved six percent, which is not only statistically significant, but the coaches figured it was worth about eight games a year."

Although the benefits of VMBR have only recently come to light, some coaches have instinctively known that concentration, relaxation, and confidence are essential for good playing. Most notably, Bob Cousy led the Boston Celtics, and coach John Wooden the UCLA Bruins, to many victories using this type of conditioning. Long-term confidence is probably the hardest of these traits to instill. Coaches successful in this endeavor can influence not only a player's skills on the court, but his or her personal life. On a nonprofessional level, ultrasuccessful writer James Michener believes his basketball coach kept him out of juvenile detention homes. "In coach Grady's court we won championships and I came to regard myself a champion. I carried myself a little taller, worked a little harder in school, built a confidence that was crucial. I drew away from the boys who were headed for reform school and patterned myself after those who were headed for college." Kareem Abdul-Jabbar believes Coach Wooden was instrumental in his own success, not only as a basketball player but also as a person.

Certainly no one can argue with Kareem's success on the court. Besides having played the longest of anyone in the NBA (20 years), he holds the title for most points made (38,387), most games played (1,560), most times voted Most Valuable Player (six for NBA regular seasons), and most seasons played in the NBA play-offs (18).

One of Kareem's most popular shots was the skyhook—the ultimate hook shot. Significantly, he used it to make his record-setting thirty-eight thousandth career point. Played with his back to the basket, the shot added grace and excitement to any game. "The skyhook has definite advantages," he says. "I don't have to rely on brute force or blinding speed to utilize it. It doesn't require a good pass, but if you're moving when you get one, it's easy to shoot it before anybody can react. You grasp the ball, take a step, coil, launch yourself into the air, extend your arm, lengthen your body, and then release the ball. You can't defend against it; nobody can get a hand on it—I can shoot it over Manute Bol. Practicing the hook shot improved not only the mechanics of the shot, but also my overall concentration. Shooting it is a very Zen activity: You center on your inner calm and your target, isolating everything else until you and your objective become one."

There goes Kareem, using the right side of his brain again!

Chapter 3

Bicycling

Design and Performance

"I believe that cycling is the toughest sport of all, and if I'm at the top of one of the toughest sports, then I've got to be one of the top American athletes."

—*Greg LeMond, Three-time winner of the Tour de France*

I t's hard to quantify the impact cycling has had on western civilization. Sir Arthur Conan Doyle developed many of his Sherlock Holmes stories while cycling with his wife on their two-person tricycle. Perhaps even more important, the women's movement took great strides when ladies refused to heed advice given in the June 5, 1890, edition of *Woman:* "Few will contend that the lady cyclist is a thing of beauty. The pedal action is too like the rhythmic swing of a carpet beater, and the addition of dust to a heated face and shapeless garments in no way suggests personal cleanliness."

Apparently, women didn't care: they shortened their skirts by a few inches, weighted down the hems with lead, and took to the road. Now they even compete in the Tour de France and get their opinions polled. (A recent survey in *Bicycling* magazine showed that men tend to think of sex while bicycling and women think of bicycling while having sex.) Quite a change from the attitudes of a century ago.

Besides providing fun and great exercise for both men and women, cycling is the most efficient means of transportation ever invented. Pound for pound and calorie for calorie, no other mode is as efficient. It has become the most popular recreational sport in America—with 85 million participants, 20 million of whom bicycle at least once a week.

What Makes a Bike Go

The amount of power generated by a cyclist depends largely on muscle mass, body weight, and body fat. On a professional level, endurance racers tend to be lighter (140–160 pounds) than sprinters (200 pounds plus). On long-haul runs, endurance depends more on the amount of oxygen absorbed into the system than on pure muscle mass.

A cyclist's legs provide the mechanical leverage, which translates into torque **(see Figure 3-1)**. As a knee straightens to pedal, the quadricep muscle on the front of the thigh contracts. A contracting muscle can exert as much as 100 pounds of pressure per square inch of its cross-sectional area. In that quadriceps can have an area as large as 16 square inches, theoretically, up to 1,600 pounds of force is possible.

3-1   *Torque. A cyclist's legs provide the mechanical leverage known as torque. As the knee straightens to pedal, the quadriceps muscle located on the front of the thigh contracts.*

On a bicycle, a chain and gearing system transmit the power from the pedals to the wheels. If you likened a cyclist's power system to that of an automobile, the rider would be the fuel system, the pedal action a camshaft, the chain a drivertrain, and the gears a transmission. But a bicycle uses energy considerably more efficiently than an automobile engine. Just compare it with some other modes of transportation: a salmon uses two and a half more calories to move the same amount of weight the same distance, a jet four times as much, a walking person five times, and a helicopter more than 200 times.

Measured in horsepower, mechanical power is the result of torque and speed over time. One horsepower equals 550 foot-pounds per second (ft-lb/sec), 33,000 foot-pounds per minute (ft-lb/min), or 746 watts. In other words, one horsepower is the force required to raise 500 pounds one foot in one second—quite a feat of strength. The term horsepower was coined by James Watt in 1783 in comparing the working capacity of his steam engine to strong work horses. By experimenting with London's strongest draft horses, he found that during an 8-hour day a horse could work at a rate of 22,000 ft-lb/min. Somewhat arbitrarily, he conservatively increased the 22,000 figure by 50 percent to 33,000 ft-lb/min, and defined this power as one horsepower (hp).

It is possible for a very strong athlete to generate 5 hp for a movement taking less than a second. For activities lasting five minutes, the same person may be able to generate 2 hp. For longer periods, one-half hp is a major production of power. In 1975 Eddy Merckx produced more than 0.6 hp for an hour. (He was the first cyclist in history to win the Triple Crown of bicycling—in 1974 he won the Tour of Italy, the Tour de France, and the World Road Championship.)

Lengthening crank distance can increase pedal torque. Too far, however, and the legs quickly tire. Also, both legs are not equally efficient. The Japanese Research Institute found that one leg can often produce 10 percent more or less power than the other.

The human power plant is an amazing piece of equipment, and develops power through these steps:

- Blood cells absorb oxygen from the lungs.
- In the muscle cells, glucose combines with this oxygen to form adenosine triphosphate, and with fatty acids to make phosphocreatine. These two compounds liberate energy as needed by the human body. To a point, they are produced as quickly as needed to sustain the muscles' demand for energy.
- For a moderate workout, the glucose needed to energize the muscles comes chiefly from the breakdown of fat. As the energy requirement intensifies, more of the glucose is taken from stored carbohydrates, until reaching an upper level, when the entire supply comes from carbohydrates.

The body is quite inefficient compared with a bicycle. During a workout, three-quarters of the food eaten and oxygen absorbed is spent either on heating or cooling the body. Only 10 to 25 percent converts into energy for muscular work and other bodily functions. Theoretically, each liter of oxygen should enable us to produce 0.4 hp; in reality, it usually only produces about 0.1 hp. Training can make our bodies more efficient, however.

What Makes a Bike Slow Down

As efficient as a bicycle is, lovers of the sport are always trying to make it even better and that means getting rid of friction. Of all the forces reducing mechanical efficiency, friction takes the largest toll. On a bicycle, these forces are axle friction, rolling resistance, chain resistance, and, the most substantial, air and wind resistance.

Axle Friction
Bearing friction can absorb anywhere from 3 to 10 percent of the energy output, depending on the level of adjustment and on the amount and type of lubricant. Chester R. Kyle, Ph.D., science editor for *Bicycling*, tested three types of bearings for friction: cone-and-cup, sealed, and shielded bearings. Kyle is noted for his expertise on the science and mechanics of bicycles. Not only has he been involved personally with

testing many bicycle components (he helped build and design some of the components and frames used by U.S. riders in the 1984 Olympics and later world championships), he is also a cofounder of the International Human-Powered Vehicle Association.

Kyle's experiments on bearings included replacing bearing grease with light oil and removing the seals on sealed bearings. The most "frictionless" condition resulted with a finely adjusted cone-and-cup bearing using light grease. Coming in second was the sealed bearing with both seals removed and the grease replaced with light oil. (When finely adjusted, a bearing will run free but won't rattle.) Kyle cautions that the use of light oil should be confined to time trials or track events because the thinner oil's protection is short-lived.

Rolling Resistance

Rolling resistance develops from the contact between the tire and the surface it is up against. Energy is lost both in compressing the tire as it meets the road surface and in the subsequent expansion as it leaves the surface. The tire's attempt to form itself to the pattern of the surface also takes energy. Turning, because it increases the amount of surface contact area, increases the resistance. Smaller wheels produce more resistance, regardless of the size of tire, because they are more sensitive to the surface roughness and are subject to more deformation.

Anything that reduces the surface area contact between the tire and road will also reduce the amount of resistance and subsequently increase a cyclist's speed. The easiest modification available is to increase air pressure in the tire. Thinner, more flexible tires also decrease resistance (natural latex more so than synthetic butyl rubber). Except for the most expensive tubulars, clincher tires generally have less friction.

The coefficient of rolling resistance on asphalt for tubular tires ranges from 0.22 to 0.59 (as a percentage of the load placed on the wheel). For clinchers, the range is 0.27 to 0.39. Total rolling resistance is computed by multiplying this coefficient by the weight (bicycle and rider) and dividing by 100. Generally, this figure falls between a half and one pound. As weight increases, so does rolling resistance.

Chain Friction

The chain remains one of the bike's most efficient components. The least amount of friction occurs with chains that are somewhat worn and that are lubricated with a light oil. Under these conditions only about 2 percent of the energy is lost. The small amount of friction generated is primarily due to the links resisting a rotating movement as they advance onto the sprocket.

As the chain's spins and bushings wear, elongation of the links occurs. Chain company engineers recommend a 1-percent limit on wearing, with 3 percent considered intolerable. (The chain will jump teeth when the percentage of stretch equals 200 divided by the number of teeth.)

If a new chain does not receive additional lubrication, the 3-percent wear limit generally happens in about 1,500 miles. If, on the other hand, it is properly maintained (cleaned and oiled after each eight hours of use), the chain should last ten times as long. Also, friction is minimized. Heavier lubricants last longer but cause more friction.

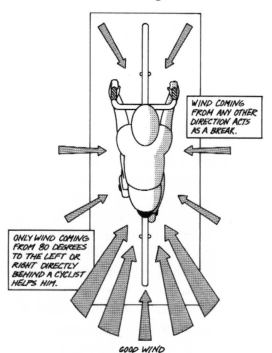

WIND COMING FROM ANY OTHER DIRECTION ACTS AS A BREAK.

ONLY WIND COMING FROM 80 DEGREES TO THE LEFT OR RIGHT DIRECTLY BEHIND A CYCLIST HELPS HIM.

GOOD WIND

3-2 *How Wind Can Help or Hinder a Cyclist. Only wind coming from 80 degrees to the left or right from behind a cyclist helps him. Wind coming from any other direction acts as a brake.*

Wind Resistance

Air resistance slows down a cyclist more than any other factor. In calm air at 20 mph, wind resistance produces a braking force of 4 to 5 pounds; at 30 mph, this resistance quickly increases to 9 to 20 pounds.

Because the retarding force of air resistance increases as the square of the velocity, and the power to overcome this resistance is drag force multiplied by velocity, the energy needed to overcome air resistance increases proportionately to the velocity cubed. Traveling at 10 mph on a level road, a cyclist uses 50 percent of his power to overcome air resistance; at speeds above 25 mph, this percentage increases to 90 percent! (A streamlined, enclosed recumbent can eliminate seven-eighths of this drag.)

According to scientist Kyle and other researchers, only wind coming from 80 degrees to the left or right from behind a cyclist helps him. Wind coming from any other direction will act as a brake **(see Figure 3–2)**.

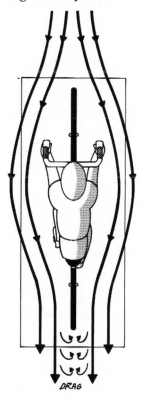

3-3 *How Air Flows Around a Cyclist. The pressure of air resistance is high in front of the cyclist and low behind him, the difference between the two producing a drag force perpendicular to the cyclist's body.*

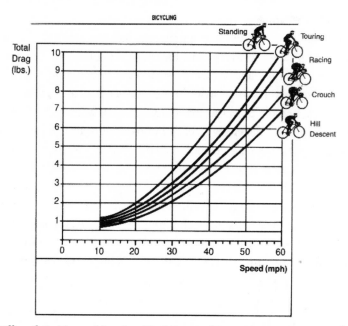

3-4 *Effect of Position and Speed on Total Drag and Power. Because 70 percent of drag comes from the cyclist's body surface, a cyclist's position can markedly affect efficiency. A crouched position can lower wind resistance by as much as 30 percent.*

The component of wind resistance having the most effect is pressure drag. When a surface faces the wind, higher pressures occur in front of it and lower pressures behind it. The resulting pressure difference produces a drag force perpendicular to the surface **(see Figure 3–3)**.

The largest amount of drag (about 70 percent) occurs from the cyclist's body surface. Therefore, the position maintained can markedly affect efficiency. A crouched position can lower wind resistance by as much as 30 percent **(see Figure 3–4)**. According to Kyle, a crouched cyclist requires about 160 watts (0.21 hp), to go 20 mph, versus 200 watts (0.27 hp) to go the same speed in an upright position. Translated into road speed, an upright rider can lose as much as 3 mph. Loose clothing can cause an additional 30-percent increase in drag.

"Drafting" is a technique of using the slipstream of another rider to increase speed (or at least decrease effort). By staying in the "wind shadow" of the rider in front, a cyclist can save a large amount of energy (about 30 percent). A couple or group riding together can take advantage of this phenomenon by rotating the lead position.

Motorpacing is a variation of drafting. By following a motorcycle or car that shelters a bike from air resistance, a cyclist can achieve amazing speeds. The current record of 152.28 mph was set in 1985 by John Howard of Encinitas, California, on the Bonneville Salt Flats. A former Olympic cyclist, he rode a 46-pound, specially designed bike that used motorcycle tires.

Important aerodynamic improvements have been made in bicycle designs that effectively reduce wind resistance. Disk wheels, three-spoke aerodynamic wheels, and aero bars are among the improvements. Kyle, by experimenting in wind tunnels, found that at 30 mph, disk wheels can eliminate 150 grams of drag. These wheels typically cost from $500 to $1,000 each, so for most cyclists the cost doesn't justify the seconds saved. In the big leagues, however, it's important. Greg LeMond won the 23-day, 2,025-mile Tour-de-France in 1989 by just eight seconds. His bike had one disk wheel; second place finisher Fignon's had two. (Apparently winning does take something more than just good wheels!)

Kyle also tested a three-spoke aerodynamic wheel. Not as affected by crosswinds as the disk wheels, it is in some respects superior, in that drag rates are similar. The wheel is, however, illegal for international racing.

On a regular spoked wheel, drag can be almost halved by using flat, aerodynamically shaped spokes. However, the cost and difficulty of installing the spokes is likely to keep them from capturing a large audience.

Aero bars, a somewhat recent development, are rapidly gaining in popularity. The bars allow the rider to rest on the elbows; hands can be clasped in front. Not only is the position comfortable but, if the seat is correctly adjusted, the cyclist's back will be kept flat and the elbows tucked in—positions conducive to reduced air resistance. Most riders see an immediate 1- to 2-mph increase in speed. Because the extended position maintained by the rider puts more weight on the front wheel, steering is quicker and front brakes are more sensitive. It takes a few hours of riding to adapt to the new position. Clip-on models are available **(see Figure 3–5)**.

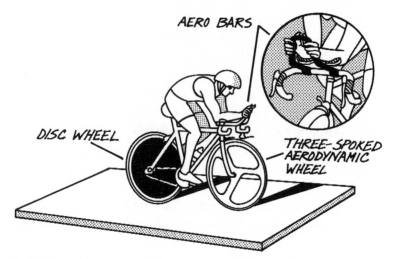

3-5 *Cyclists' Aids. Aerodynamics improvements designed to reduce wind resistance include disc wheel, aero-bars, and three-spoke wheels.*

Weight

Although extra pounds help a cyclist go faster downhill, those same pounds unfortunately must be lugged uphill. Also, more weight increases the rolling resistance a cyclist encounters.

Because parts of it rotate, the forward motion of a bicycle requires more energy than moving a solid block of the same weight. (Energy is required both for the spin and the forward motion.) Therefore, one pound on the wheel of a bicycle has the same effect as two pounds on the frame. Kyle's computer modeling showed that extra weight particularly impacts hill climbing or accelerating in the wrong gear.

Slopes

Hills are an obvious impediment to speed. Consider this: If a rider is maintaining 10 mph on a ten-speed touring bike, he must generate 0.055 hp on a flat grade. On a 5-percent grade, to maintain the same speed he must generate 0.22 hp; on a 10-percent grade, 0.43 hp; and on a 25-percent grade, more than 1 hp. These numbers put Merckx's record achievement in better perspective: when he generated 0.6 hp for an hour, it was the equivalent of riding up a 15-percent grade at 10 mph.

Braking

Braking is one type of friction where "more is better." The greater the friction, the quicker the stop. The years have seen an improvement in the material used for brakes, which, when coupled with aluminum rims, has greatly improved stopping power.

A good rule of thumb for checking brakes: On dry pavement, a rider going 15 mph should be able to stop in 10 to 14 feet. On wet pavement, this distance should increase by only 3 or 4 feet.

Front brakes applied too forcefully result in an-oops-"face plant" as the rider pitches forward over the handlebars. Consequently, many riders avoid using the front brake much, which is also a mistake. Although the rear wheel normally carries 50 to 60 percent of the weight, when brakes are applied, some of the weight shifts forward, so both brakes must be applied for an efficient stop (but only when traveling in a straight line). To avoid face plants while braking hard, the buttocks should slide backward on the saddle—the harder the stop, the more distance back.

The idea in braking is to keep the center of gravity in the middle of the bike as much as possible. The mere act of decelerating transfers weight toward the front. Therefore, if both brakes are applied and the rear wheel skids, easing off the front pressure effectively transfers more of the weight to the back wheel. (Practice is required because the inclination is to do the opposite.)

Cadence

Cadence describes the speed at which the pedals turn. Hobby cyclists customarily ride in a high gear at 50 to 60 revolutions per minute (rpm) whereas racers and those cycling for fitness go from 80 to 110 rpm in the middle gears. In this range, the cadence is called spinning. A higher cadence produces more power. At lower revolutions, more of the cyclist's energy goes toward turning the pedals, and much energy is required just to increase speed.

Although many exercise physiologists advise pedaling slower in higher gears, performance cyclists seldom take that advice. Dr. Peter

Maude and his co-workers at the Human Movement Laboratory at Eastern Washington University ran a test for both competitive and recreational cyclists for 60-minute rides (longer than those used in previous studies) to see which speed was most efficient.

For recreational cyclists, the physiologists proved right. Riders became less efficient when pedaling faster and required significantly more oxygen. However, the competition cyclists were equally efficient in either mode.

High performers probably feel more comfortable with a faster cadence because there is less resistance with each stroke, and because more blood flow (and hence more oxygen) can circulate, in that the muscles aren't contracting as hard. (Heavy contractions can interfere with blood flow.) This speed also allows the cyclist to use the so-called "aerobic" (slow-twitch) muscle fibers, which are more fatigue resistant.

An earlier efficiency study done at the Japanese Bicycle Research Institute tested four cyclists at various speeds and gearing. Oxygen consumption determined efficiency. Pedal speeds found most efficient were:

Table 3-1
Optimum Pedal Speeds per Bike Speed

BIKE SPEED (MPH)	PEDAL SPEED (RPM)
12	42
15	49
18	61-66
21	65-70

Both of these studies used small samples. However, the data are consistent. Clearly, the key to efficiency is for a cyclist to gradually work up to a higher cadence.

Human-Powered Vehicles (HPVs) and Recumbents

In that cycling is one of the most efficient forms of transportation, it is not surprising that other forms of locomotion have adapted its principles. The following are among the most notable.

Helicopters

Human-powered copters have long intrigued designers and cycling aficionados. Both the Japanese and English have made numerous attempts
to build them. Two awards are available to the team that ultimately succeeds: the American Helicopter Society Award ($10,000) and the
Smithsonian Award ($100,000). The winning helicopter must rise
immediately to at least three meters and stay aloft for at least one
minute.

At this time, the odds are on a team from California Polytechnic
State University. Builders Neal Saiki and Kyle Naydo's *Da Vinci III*
recently rose seven inches off the floor and stayed aloft for 6.8 seconds.
The helicopter weighed a mere 97 pounds, and its 100-foot rotor spun at
about 8 rpm. The pilot, Greg McNeil, weighed 127 pounds and had to
generate more than 1 hp to get the bird off the ground.

Now under construction is *Da Vinci IV*, which will have a 120-foot
rotor and should weigh only about 75 pounds. The team believes these
changes will allow the copter to stay aloft for a minute if McNeil generates 0.7 hp.

A motorized helicopter is one of the least efficient modes of transportation, having 200 times the energy requirement, pound for pound,
of a bicycle. These teams are tackling quite a challenge.

Submarines

California Polytechnic is also making its mark in human-powered sub-
marines. In June 1989, their *Submersion* won a 100-meter sprint in a
Florida contest sponsored by the H. A. Perry Foundation and Florida
Atlantic University. The fiberglass submarine averaged 2.94 mph, but
was slowed down by turbulent water.

Hydrofoils

Awards give an added impetus to technical projects, and to that end
DuPont is particularly generous. Among the many awards the company
has offered is one for $25,000 to the first human-powered watercraft that
exceeds 20 knots (23 mph) over a 100-meter course.

Coming close to winning was Bobby Livingston's human-powered hydrofoil. In September 1989, his *Flying Fish* achieved 16.1 knots (18.5 mph), thereby setting a world record.

Recumbents

Built for speed and streamlined to drastically reduce and sometimes almost eliminate air resistance, recumbents are taking the lead in HPV records. The name comes from the prone position the rider maintains while pedaling (although not so prone that he can't see ahead). Because the legs stretch out forward, added power is conveyed to the pedals. More of the energy output goes for forward motion, and less used to stay upright as on a regular bicycle. A low center of gravity also improves cornering abilities. Fairings are frequently used, which are plastic shields built in front of, and sometimes completely surrounding, the rider.

The record speed achieved by a cyclist unpaced and unaided by wind was made in 1986 by Fred Markham. Scorching along Big Sand Flat in California on May 12, Markham pedaled his 31-pound, covered recumbent *Gold Rush* to 65.48 mph. The fairing used DuPont's Kevlar and, to lighten the load, almost all steel parts were replaced with titanium or aluminum. Markham's speed was calculated over 200 meters. It took him about two minutes to get up to top speed. DuPont had offered an $18,000 award to the first cyclist to break 65 mph, which Markham and his designer, Gardner Martin, shared.

IHPVA

In 1975, a group of HPV enthusiasts, frustrated with the bans imposed by the International Cycling Union (UCI), founded the International Human-Powered Vehicle Association (IHPVA). One ruling that particularly incensed them made illegal all innovations that serve only to streamline a vehicle (such as fairings). IHPVA believes that such bans ultimately inhibit the development of technological improvements that could help all cyclists. Therefore, they formed their own group and set out to be the fastest on the road, using any modern technology available. Since the Association's inception, members of the group have broken many speed records.

The Daedalus Project

"We've just lost sight of land—another first for human powered aircraft!" shouted the flight controller from his inflatable. This remarkable 3-hour, 54-minute flight then went on to set records in distance, speed, and endurance.

Nothing has made the hearts of HPV enthusiasts soar so high as the *Daedalus 88* making its human-powered flight across the Aegean Sea on April 23, 1988. The 72-mile journey from Crete to the island of Santorini was a triumph of technology, biochemistry, and aeronautics. Daedalus's flight exceeded by 50 miles the previous record for a human-powered flight, made by the *Gossamer Albatross* across the English Channel in 1979.

The team behind the project hoped to recreate the Greek legend told by Ovid and Apollodorus. According to this myth, Daedalus and his son Icarus escaped from the labyrinth Daedalus himself devised for the Minotaur on Crete, using wings made of wax and feathers. Sadly, Icarus flew too close to the sun and his wings melted, resulting in a quick and fatal plunge into the sea. Daedalus was more prudent and flew on to safety.

The successful flight of *Daedalus 88* was due in part to improvements made since the *Gossamer Albatross's* journey, and included graphite—epoxy composite materials, special airfoils, and an electronically controlled propeller.

According to John Langford, project manger for the flight, the team made many experiments on a prototype aircraft before completing the Daedalus. "The plane carried a dozen experiments to determine the exact power required to fly it—including measuring the torque of the propeller drive shaft and the oxygen consumption of the pilots. Chemicals painted on the wings revealed airflow patterns, which could be compared with [our] computerized predictions. These valuable experiments revealed that the plane required about 1.5 watts of power for every pound the pilot weighed: a 150-pound person would have to expend about 0.30 horsepower."

Specifications on the Daedalus are impressive:

Empty weight: 70 lbs
Gross weight: 229 lbs
Span: 112 ft
Wing area: 332 sq ft
Flight speed: 14-17 mph (with tailwinds, it actually averaged 18.9 mph)
Pilot power: About 0.27 hp

Despite the fact that *Daedalus* landed 20 feet short of its goal (and in the water), the project certainly met or exceeded expectations. The information obtained from this program had direct applications to the later design of many high altitude, long endurance aircraft.

Chapter 4
Billiards

Physics at the Pool Hall

"At the end of the game, you count up the money and that's how you know who's best."

—*George C. Scott, In* The Hustler

Tuscaloosa Squirrel, Knoxville Bear, Cornbread Red, Rotation Slim: Are these players from the San Diego Zoo? Actually, no. Try pool hustlers of note. Sharpshooters all, and smart, but mentioning Newton to them would probably bring to mind apples or figs, not ideas on how they could improve their vocations. More important to them is a good feel for a cue stick and a daring sense of salesmanship.

The terms billiards and pool are often used interchangeably, but differences do exist. Carom billiards, or simply billiards, requires a player to bank the cue ball off three or more cushions and hit two object balls in varying sequences. Pocket billiards, or pool, is the game commonly seen in pool halls around the country. Originally, players pooled money for the stakes, hence its name. Variations of each game abound. The British are partial to snooker, the three-cushion billiards; in the United States, players enjoy straight pool (15 balls), nine-ball (9 balls), eight-ball (15 balls), 14.1 continuous, and most recently seven-ball, the first fully authenticated new game in a century.

On a day when Tuscaloosa Squirrel is having a hard time making his shots, it may help him to know that three physical properties manifest themselves each time a cue ball is hit:

- The velocity of the ball is determined by the force of the stroke.
- The direction of spin is determined by the length and direction of the "lever arm" between the center of the ball and point of impact **(see Figure 4–1).**

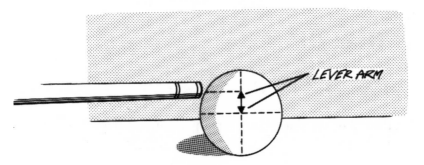

4-1 *How Lever Arm Affects Spin. The length and direction of the area between the center of the ball and the point of impact, determines the direction of the spin.*

• The rate of spin is proportionate to the torque generated by the shot and the ball's moment of inertia.

Torque is the effect of a force acting at a distance from a pivot point, and is generated only when a "lever arm" exists. If a ball is struck dead center, no torque is generated and initially the ball will only slide across the surface until friction causes it to roll. "Moment of inertia" is an effect on motion arising from an object's shape. A spinning I-beam, for example, will possess a different moment than a square block, even if their masses are the same. A spinning billiard ball, rotating around a central axis, will experience a moment of inertia equal to two-fifths its mass times its radius squared.

Friction occurs from the weight of the ball moving against the table and is highly dependent on the surface texture. Most table covers are either wool (which lasts a long time) or a nylon/wool blend. The greater the nylon content, the faster the roll.

A ball "rolls smoothly" if it is not sliding at all. Such a state occurs if the forward motion of the ball is exactly matched by the motion of the bottom surface at the point of contact with the table **(see Figure 4–2)**. Smooth rolling happens in one of two ways: (1) after slipping awhile across the table, enough friction develops to cause the ball to spin at rolling speed, or (2) the right conditions are set up initially on the shot.

In order for a cue ball to have this initial state of smooth rolling, it

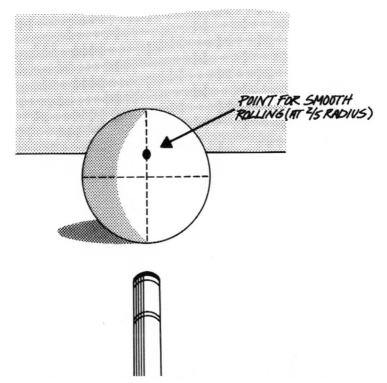

POINT FOR SMOOTH
ROLLING (AT 2/5 RADIUS)

4-2 *Point for Smooth Rolling. When the ball is hit at this point, its forward motion will exactly match the motion of the bottom surface at the point of contact with the table.*

must be hit at a precise location. This point is right above its center, at a vertical distance exactly two-fifths the radius of the ball.

The resulting two-fifths figure for the lever arm length in effect "cancels out" the two fifths used in the formula to compute the moment of inertia.

Draw and Follow

Until 1798, players always attempted to hit a cue ball dead on. Then a creative political prisoner in France, Captain Mingaud, tried putting leather on the end of the cue tip. Voila—"cue-ball magic" was born. Mingaud was so impressed with the spin exhibited by the ball that he

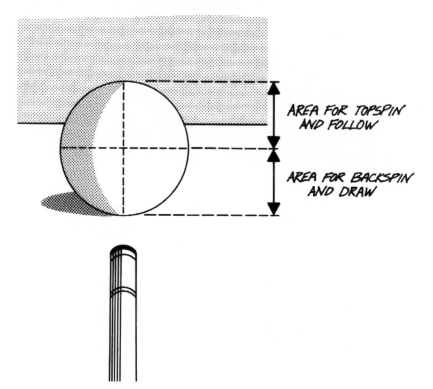

AREA FOR TOPSPIN
AND FOLLOW

AREA FOR BACKSPIN
AND DRAW

4-3 *Most Effective Striking Area. A ball hit above the center point will roll farther, and one hit below the center point will stop shorter, than a ball hit dead center.*

asked for and received an extension of his sentence so that he could practice. Experience paid off, and upon release, Mingaud went out and made his living playing the game—possibly the first professional hustler in the history of billiards.

Since that time, scientists have enthusiastically applied Newton's laws to spinning billiard balls. Although such knowledge can undoubtedly help players make more "potters" (shots put into the pocket), only practice can substantially influence how well a person does at the table. Understanding the physics of motion comes in most handy when a player, while making a potter, sets up for the next shot.

By aiming at a specific point on the cue ball, a player can manipulate the two spin planes that determine the ball's subsequent motion. If

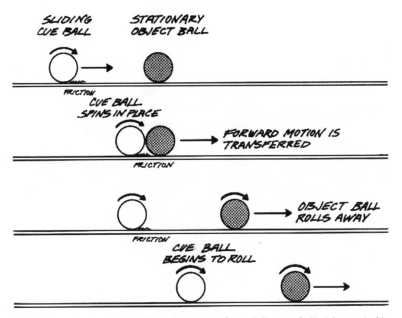

4-4 *Four Stages in a Follow Shot. A moment after a sliding cue ball with topspin hits an object ball, it begins to spin forward, or "follow," the object ball.*

the ball is hit above or below center, the horizontal plane is influenced, and if the ball is hit to the right or left of center, the vertical plane is influenced. "Draw" and "follow" occur from the first effect; "English" from the second.

Follow is the result of topspin on a ball. Frictional forces then parallel the forward motion, and contribute to the total forward force. Hence, a ball with topspin will roll farther than one without it **(see Figure 4–3)**. When a cue ball with topspin hits an object ball, and if the cue ball is still sliding (i.e., not rolling smoothly), the cue ball's center of mass will be motionless but the ball will keep spinning in place. After a moment, this rotation causes the ball again to roll forward, "following" the object ball **(see Figure 4–4)**.

Conversely, a ball with backspin slows down as it moves across the table because friction is working in a direction opposite to the forward motion. After impact with an object ball, the cue ball reverses its direction and returns toward the player, an action called draw.

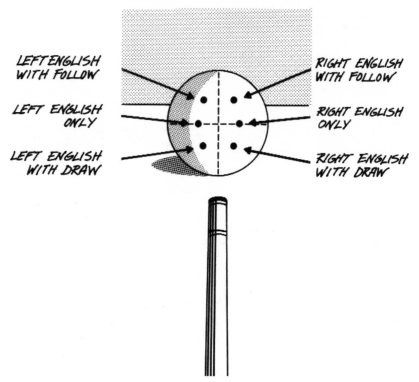

LEFT ENGLISH
WITH FOLLOW

LEFT ENGLISH
ONLY

LEFT ENGLISH
WITH DRAW

RIGHT ENGLISH
WITH FOLLOW

RIGHT ENGLISH
ONLY

RIGHT ENGLISH
WITH DRAW

4-5 *English. If a cue ball is hit to the left or right of center, its vertical spin plane is affected. During a collision, part of the cue ball's spin transfers to the object ball, making it spin in a direction opposite that of the cue ball.*

The further off center a ball is hit, the more pronounced the follow or draw. Generally, the maximum effective off-center distance is the width of the cue tip. More than that is likely to cause a miscue or missed shot. How hard and fast the cue ball is struck also affects the amount of draw or follow.

A cue ball stopping dead after it hits an object ball may seem like magic to a first-time onlooker, but the shot is easily achieved with the proper stroke. The cue ball is hit just below center, but not as low or with as much force as that used to produce draw. Upon impact, friction matches the backward spill of the ball, so no force is available to propel the ball in any direction. This stopping dead is called sticking. The distance below center at which the cue ball should be struck is proportionate to the distance to the object ball. The closer the object ball, the less distance below center the cue ball should be struck.

English

If a cue ball is hit to the left or right of center, its vertical spin plane is affected. The ball will spin one way and will travel down the table in a direction opposite its spin. The competent display of this technique, called English, identifies a well-practiced player. Supposedly the name came from an Englishman named English, who came to the United States in the latter part of the last century and who so impressed Americans with his demonstration of putting "side" on the balls that they named the effect after him. Stroking a ball on the left side gives left English, and makes the ball spin clockwise; on the right, right English and a counterclockwise spin. During a collision, part of the cue ball's spin transfers to the object ball, making it spin in a direction opposite that of the cue ball **(see Figure 4–5)**.

Natural English occurs when the cue ball is hit on the same side as the direction of the desired curve; reverse English when it is hit on the side opposite the direction it will move after it hits the rail or object ball. Natural English adds speed to the cue ball and widens the angle of the ball after impact. Reverse English slows it down and narrows the angle (and actually reverses the course the cue ball would normally travel). High English combines both English and topspin.

With practice, a player can anticipate which directions the balls should go after impact. The key is to visualize the two balls at the moment of impact and draw a line connecting their centers. The object ball will follow and extension of this line, and the cue ball will follow a path roughly perpendicular, or 90 degrees, to this line (not for those hit dead on, though).

"Frozen" balls, which are two object balls touching one another or one solidly up against the rail, require a slightly different analysis. Friction created between the object balls or the object ball and rail can significantly alter the pathway. The clearest way to see what happens is by way of example.

Immediately after the cue ball strikes the four ball, the four and six balls collide. You would expect the six ball to travel along an extension of a line drawn between the four and six ball centers, and the four ball to travel perpendicular to this line. In reality, however, the friction developed between the frozen balls causes the six ball to move perpendicular to its expected path for just an instant before it continues along its expected route. This slight adjustment (called throw) in the initial track line makes the actual pathway a few degrees to the left of what would have been anticipated. Similarly, a shot colliding with a ball snug up against the rail will encounter friction that will redirect the pathway.

Physics lessons aside, the best way to make more potters is to 1) practice, practice, practice, 2) own a good pool cue, and 3) play against people not as expert as yourself. It wouldn't hurt to take lessons from someone like Michael Eufemia, either, who holds the record for "greatest continuous run" in a straight pool match, set in 1960 when he pocketed 625 balls without a miss. Englishman Rob McKenna wouldn't be a bad teacher, either. He holds the record for pocketing all fifteen balls in the shortest time (37.9 seconds), done on November 7, 1987.

A Perfect Cue

Can a pool cue be worth $5,000? Fortunately for Bill Stroud, some people think so. Stroud custom designs and manufactures cues from his mountain workshop in Colorado Springs, Colorado. "Having your own cue and playing with it constantly adds twenty percent to your ability," he says, "and a tenth is enough to win at the top." Now a respectable businessman doing business as Joss Cues West, Stroud used to be a full-time pool hustler, until the miles wore him down. "I've been in about every city of over 200 population." In 1968, he and his partner, Danny Janes, neither of whom had used a lathe in his life, set up shop. For less than $800, they bought all the tools needed to turn out pool cues. Fine equipment it was not (the bandsaw had been used to slice meat), but that didn't prevent the team for making fine cues. The second one made sold for $85.

Today Stroud turns out sticks on a lathe that cost $27,000. Business has been good. He also uses a computer-driven industrial milling machine, which allows him to engrave elaborate designs in the pool cue butts.

What makes a good cue? Pros agree that it must be well-made, balanced, and of the right size. A handle wrapped with Irish linen is preferable to leather or rubber because perspiration is absorbed. Cues making the circuit should be in two pieces and screwed together as needed. The shaft should be made of maple or some other hardwood, and the best butts are made of ebony.

The crème de la crème of cue sticks were made by the late George Balabuska of Brooklyn, New York, and are now collectors' items. In the film *The Color of Money*, an outrageous scene had Paul Newman throwing a Balabuska across the room to Tom Cruise—shocking those who recognized the cue for what it was. As Kent Anderson, owner of Anchorage's River Billiards, says, "It would be like your wife throwing a Chinese vase from the Ming Dynasty across the living room."

The Color of Money was aptly named for several reasons. The gambling aspect of the game is obvious, but pros also use dollar bills to clean the tip and shaft of their cues. Besides removing dirt, the bills condition the stick by leaving a slightly oily, shiny surface. (Whether they use fifty-dollar bills or tens depends on how well the game is going.)

Expert Steve Mizerak recommends thoroughly conditioning a new stick after a few weeks of use. To do this he first uses a washcloth and wets the shaft with fairly warm water. Then, after it dries but while the pores are still open, he rubs lighter fluid into the shaft. This procedure fills the pores with a light oil and effectively seals the shaft. Mizerak is best known for his Miller Lite Beer commercial, where he sinks six balls in one shot **(see Figure 4–6)**. (Although the commercial took almost 11 hours to shoot, don't blame Mizerak: He has his "just showin' off" shot down pat and can usually do in on demand.)

Mizerak uses a lot of high right-hand English, and solidly drives the cue ball into the left half of the one ball. The chain reaction that follows pockets all six balls. He also places a glass of beer (Miller Lite, naturally) on the table. As the cue ball makes its way toward the six ball, he nonchalantly picks up the glass to let the cue ball pass. And just as nonchalantly says modestly, "I was just showin' off."

You won't catch Mizerak using an aluminum or fiberglass cue,

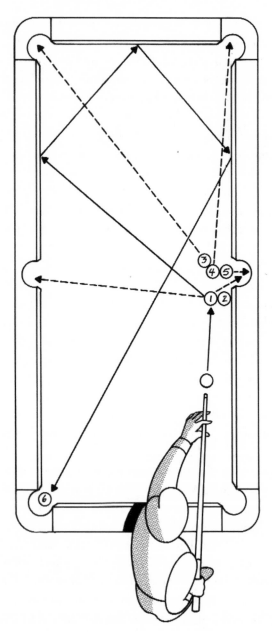

4-6 *Mizerak's Shot. The famous Miller Lite Beer commercial shot, in which Steve Miserak is "just showin' off."*

though both are available. Stroud agrees with him. "The best cues are made out of wood that's totally relaxed," says this expert cue maker. "If the tree grows on a hillside, it'll grow at a different rate on each side and that creates a lot of tension. A lot of cue makers don't have a chance to let their cues sit around and relax." He uses Canadian maple and makes sure his sticks relax: at one point in the process they "rest" for two months.

Perfect pool cues are generally 57 to 58 inches long (the pros use 58 inches), and weigh from 17 to 22 ounces. The tips are made from leather and must be a solid oval to work properly. Stroud uses special French "Champion" tips made from water buffalo hide. This material hasn't been available since the late sixties, but Stroud pulled a coup when he bought a large supply years ago. He also uses elephant ivory for the furls, but from ivory taken before he was born. "I'm a member of Greenpeace, and I think ivory looks better on the elephant than it does on ladies' hands or on a pool cue."

Chapter 5
The Boomerang

Gyroscopic Precession and the Return Home

"The boomerang is a wonderful invention that starts out in one spot, faithfully returns, and makes a lovely flight of fancy in between. It's hard not to admire a piece of wood that can find its own way home."
—*Stephen S. Hall*

Grasping the boomerang by one end, the pitcher arches his arm behind him and with a quick forward motion and snap of the wrist hurls the boomerang into the air. Moving at roughly 60 mph and spinning end over end at about 10 revolutions per minute, the boomerang gracefully turns left and makes incremental adjustments until it lies on its side; pulsating and swishing through the air it completes a slow, easy circle and lands at the thrower's feet. If conditions are just right, the 'rang makes a second loop before landing—figure eight in the sky.

The boomerang's flight pattern has long held a fascination for physicists and scientists; frustration, too. "It's harder to analyze the flight of a boomerang than it is a flight to the moon and back," say those who know and have done both. Few other devices are subject to so many physical phenomena working at the same time. To clearly understand the principles, it helps to visualize the process in three dimensions.

Two major attributes contribute to the boomerang's return home: wings shaped like an airfoil generate lift similar to an airplane's wing, and a rapid spinning motion makes it subject to gyroscopic forces. A gyroscope is simply an object or wheel rapidly spinning around a free axis. Anytime such an object spins, it develops rotational inertia, or angular momentum. If it is gyroscopically stable, it will tend to continue spinning in the absence of any forces greater than its spinning inertia.

A gyroscopically stable object is also subject to an effect called precession. To picture this phenomenon, imagine a top rapidly spinning. At the beginning, the top maintains a perfectly upright position, but after a second or two the top of the top begins to veer away from the center axis and to describe a circle traversing around the center axis. As the top slows down, this circle becomes larger and larger, until the top falls over.

This circular motion about the vertical axis is precession, the result of incremental changes in angular momentum. With a boomerang, these incremental changes occur primarily from three forces acting on it: lift, drag, and torque.

The most obvious force acting on a boomerang is lift. Similar to an airplane wing in design, the boomerang's arms form an airfoil that forces the air flowing on top of the wing to go faster than the air below. Daniel Bernoulli, in 1738, developed laws governing this phenomenon, one of which states, in effect, that air traveling at faster speeds creates less air pressure than does air traveling at slower speeds. Consequently, on an airfoil the high-pressure zone at the bottom of the wing "pushes" the wing upward toward the low-pressure zone, thus generating lift.

Besides encountering this lifting force, the boomerang is affected by torsional effects that develop from its rotational spin. Torque is the result of a force acting through a distance and that tends to make a body rotate. On a boomerang this torque can roughly be broken into two components: one that is parallel to the velocity vector and one that is perpendicular. (A vector is a line value that includes both magnitude and direction.) The torque parallel to the velocity vector causes the 'rang to turn left; the one perpendicular causes it to "lie down."

Torsional effects occur because the leading edge of the forward-spinning arm is moving faster and is therefore subject to greater air pressure differences than that on the following arm. Imagine one of the boomerang arms being at its highest possible position and the other at its lowest. The upper arm is turning in the same direction as the forward motion, but the lower arm is moving opposite to the motion of the center.

Since air pressure differences are proportional to air speeds, the forward arm experiences greater pressure differences, and hence more lift, than the following arm. This difference in lift between the two arms causes a rotation of the boomerang's spin plane about a vertical axis, and this spin plane experiences precessional force that becomes stronger

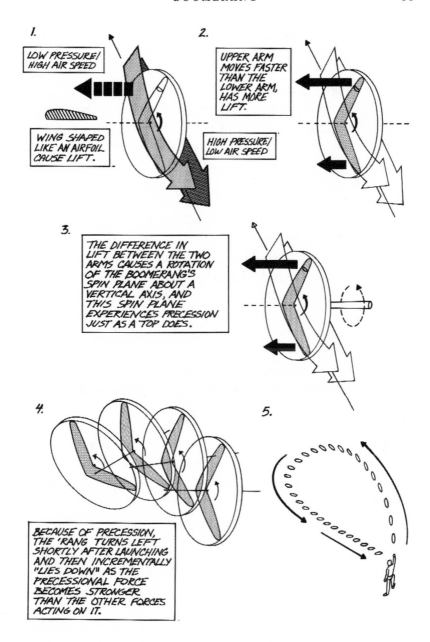

1.

LOW PRESSURE/
HIGH AIR SPEED

WING SHAPED
LIKE AN AIRFOIL
CAUSE LIFT.

2.

UPPER ARM
MOVES FASTER
THAN THE
LOWER ARM,
HAS MORE
LIFT.

HIGH PRESSURE/
LOW AIR SPEED

3.

THE DIFFERENCE IN
LIFT BETWEEN THE TWO
ARMS CAUSES A ROTATION
OF THE BOOMERANG'S
SPIN PLANE ABOUT A
VERTICAL AXIS, AND
THIS SPIN PLANE
EXPERIENCES PRECESSION
JUST AS A TOP DOES.

4.

BECAUSE OF PRECESSION,
THE 'RANG TURNS LEFT
SHORTLY AFTER LAUNCHING
AND THEN INCREMENTALLY
"LIES DOWN" AS THE
PRECESSIONAL FORCE
BECOMES STRONGER
THAN THE OTHER FORCES
ACTING ON IT.

5.

5-1 *How the Boomerang Works.*

than the other forces acting on it. By the time it returns to the thrower, the spin plane of the boomerang is more or less horizontal and the lift is almost entirely upward, so it gyrates like a helicopter fluttering toward the ground **(see Figure 5-1)**.

Although most players don't involve themselves in the physics of the boomerang, some do feel an overwhelming urge to explain the motion behind the magic. Felix Hess can claim credit for producing the granddaddy of all studies, which he titled *Boomerangs: Aerodynamics and Motion*, published in 1973. Used for his Ph.D. thesis, the report is 555 pages long.

Hess used a computer model to project various flight paths, including that taken by a boomerang launched from an aerial balloon high up in the air. The model showed that the 'rang would initially make a circle just as it would on the ground, then after free-falling for a while would enter into another circle approximating the original orbit. As Benjamin Ruhe describes it: "Taking energy from gravity, it spins and spins in a free-fall that resembles the autumnal plunge of a maple seed pod."

According to Hess, the diameter of a boomerang's orbit depends on the shape of the 'rang (because this defines its moment of inertia), and not on the forward or rotational velocity. Therefore, as long as it is thrown with sufficient velocity to complete its loop, a harder or faster throw won't make the 'rang carve out a larger circle.

Not content with this limitation, some experimenters have added ballast to the arms near the tips, finding that distance can be greatly increased. This added distance results from an increase in the moment of inertia. The ballast must be countersunk into the material, however, or it will affect the aerodynamics of the flight.

One area that neither Hess nor any other scientist has adequately studied is the effect of wake on a boomerang's path. Hess believes that the impact could be considerable, particularly as it affects the "lying down" process. This is probably a project for another graduate physics student, in that Hess has finally rid his system of the bug—at last report he was studying the mating calls of the Papua-New Guinea frog.

While still in the throes of writing his thesis, however, Hess also published an article in the November, 1968, *Scientific American*, which was quite likely responsible for the 'rang craze that developed shortly thereafter. Americans' current preoccupation with health and fitness, however, could cause the boomerang to lose favor. As Ali Fujino-Miller, past president of the U.S. Boomerang Association, puts it: "Boomeranging is the fat man's sport. The better you get, the less you have to move."

Not so with the prehistoric users of the boomerang's ancestor. Known as a "killer stick," and curved like a 'rang, it was thrown at birds and game but was generally less efficient than a bow and arrow. It didn't return home, either. The world's oldest boomerang (but probably a killer stick) was discovered in 1987 in southern Poland, and is believed to be 23,000 years old. Many reindeer bones were found buried close by, so apparently a properly shaped and thrown stick could dispatch game of some size. Scientists are unlikely to risk throwing this banana-shaped and quite fragile treasure in the air to see if it comes home. At least five continents have yielded similar finds, although not nearly as old, and most are probably killer sticks rather than boomerangs.

Surprisingly, the aerodynamics behind these sticks are even more complex than those for a returning boomerang. A good killer stick is thrown with a sidearm motion, travels at waist height, and can journey up to 200 yards. The horizontal lift must be almost entirely eliminated while enough vertical lift is maintained to hold the stick up—a difficult balance to achieve. (A boomerang, on the other hand, must be thrown vertically, not sidearm or underarm. Too much of a horizontal angle, or "layover," and it will soar upward, stall, and come crashing back down—you might call it a "booberang.")

'Rangs come in many shapes and size, but usually measure between 12 and 18 inches from tip to tip, 1½ to 2 inches wide, and ¼ to ½ inch thick. The angle between the arms varies from 70 to 140 degrees. Typical weight is about 3½ ounces **(see Figures 5–2a & b)**. The best material is Baltic birch in a marine or aircraft plywood with at least five laminations, although most builders use a premium-grade cabinetmaker's plywood. Quite varied shapes have successfully flown, including those fashioned from all of the letters of the alphabet except B, D, I, O, P and Q. And the boomerang isn't limited to two arms; extraordinary

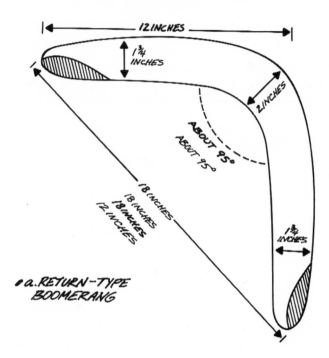

5-2a *Return Versus Non-Return-Type Boomerang. Above a return- type boomerang has 12"-long "wingspans" and measures 18" from tip to tip.*

shows have been put on using multibladers such as pinwheels. Although extravagant shapes are fun to design and experiment with, a thrower would be wise to heed the words of Rusty Harding, who manufacturers 'rangs in Tennessee: "Remember—while you are the thrower, you are also the target."

Alan Adler, who in the early seventies created the Aerobie Flying Ring (which not only improved on the Frisbee but won a place in the Guinness record book for the longest throw of any inert object heavier than air—1,257 feet) has designed and taken to market an improved boomerang he calls the Orbiter. Made of plastic and covered with soft rubber to make it friendlier to catch, the 'rang has flaps on the vertexes (intersection of the arms) to improve its aerodynamics. Lightweight, it tips the scales at two ounces. Both the Orbiter and sales have soared.

Whether a boomeranger gets joy from throwing the simplest 'rang

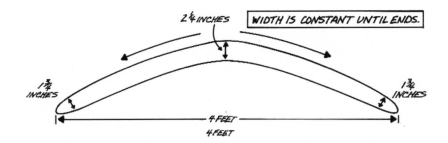

b. NON-RETURN-TYPE BOOMERANG

5-2b *Return Versus Non-Return-Type Boomerang. Above, the non-return-type boomerang used by the Australian bushmen for hunting and warfare measures 4 feet from tip to tip and weighs 3¼ pounds.*

or becomes enthralled over lighted, flapped models, this ancient sport is here to stay. Benjamin Ruhe, is his book *Boomerang*, quotes an Australian Aboriginal legend that poignantly catches the magic of the game.

In the early days of the Dreamtime, people had to crawl on their hands and knees because the sky was nearly touching the ground. An old chief came to a magic pool and stooped down to drink. As he did so, he saw a beautiful straight stick in the water and he reached in and picked it up. Then he suddenly thought, "I can push up the sky with this stick and we'll be able to stand up." So he pushed until the sky was where it is today, and the trees began to grow and the possums ran about in the branches and the kangaroos started hopping for joy. Then he looked at his stick and saw it was terribly bent. Thinking it was no good, he threw it away but it came back to him. He tried again and it came back again. So he kept the stick and called it the boomerang.

Chapter 6
Darts

Deep Elbow Bending at the Bar

"Darts is one of the most exciting indoor sports you can play with your clothes on."

—*From* All About Darts

The Crafty Cockney and his sidekick, Goldfinger, met at The Foaming Quart and he, after quaffing a Carlsberg lager, practiced the game that was to eventually earn him more than $250,000 a year. In keeping with British tradition, Eric Bristow, his real name, consistently played a serious game of darts. His dedication through the years has earned him not only a respectable livelihood but an entry in the *Guinness Book of World Records* for winning the most titles in the game.

Although the British have for centuries considered playing a good dart game akin to national patriotism, Americans have only in the last twenty years provided the Brits with serious competition. However, as is typical, when we take up a new interest we do so with a vengeance. The National Sporting Goods Association estimates that at least 12 million Americans now play darts.

Many varieties of the game exist, especially in England, but in America, the advent of the electronic dart board has served to standardize the game for most players.

The Standard U.S. Game

Each player is given a set number of points (e.g., 301, 501, 801). Scoring is a reversal of the norm; the original points are played down until none are left. On the last throw, a player must throw the exact number of his or her remaining points. Rules vary, but some games require that a "double" be hit both on the first and last throw. Although theoretically a person can finish a game of 501 by throwing only nine darts, few people in the world are that skilled.

The Dart Board and Scoring

The shape of a dart board and the pattern painted on its face can vary tremendously from pub to pub. Again, the electronic dart board and international competition have, in the last decade or so, standardized many aspects of both the board and game.

Today, we most commonly see the "clock" board, which in the United States is 18 inches in diameter, with a 13¼ inch playing area. Number 20 resides at the top. The board made to withstand the hardest use is the bristle board. These boards are manufactured by a patented process using sisal, a fiber commonly used in the making of twine. A strong, natural fiber, sisal comes from the leaves of an agave century plant (native to southern Mexico and now cultivated throughout the tropics).

The manufacturer wraps the sisal in brown paper and then slices it like a salami. The resulting wafers, or biscuits, are subjected to more than 10 tons of pressure. Each board contains about fifty biscuits. Because bristle boards are "organic," the manufacturers spray fungicide on them to deter mold and mildew.

Most American dart boards have a double-value outer ring, a treble-value inner ring, and a single and double bull's-eye **(see Figure 6–1)**. If the dart hits either of the added-value rings (and stays), the scores shown at the edge of the board are either doubled or tripled, as appropriate. The outside scoring numbers range from 1 to 20, so the maximum point value available from any one throw is 60 (i.e., 20 x 3). Bulls (bull's-eyes) count 50 points for the inner eye or circle, 25 for the outer.

Just as computers have replaced ticker tapes on Wall Street, so have electronic dart boards replaced traditional blackboard and chalk for keeping score. Some pubs still use the old method, and enjoy a colorful ambience as a result.

50-POINT
50-POINT RING
(BULL'S EYE)

25-POINT
RING

TRIPLE-SCORE
RING

DOUBLE-SCORE
RING

SINGLE-SCORE
RING

NO SCORE

6-1 *A Typical Dart Board. Most American dart boards have a double-value outer ring, a treble-value inner ring, and a single and double bull's eye.*

Darts

"Particular" describes how pro darters feel about their equipment. Shape is important—whether short, long, fat, or grooved—as is the material of the dart and the cut of the "flight," or feathers.

The barrel on a dart provides extra weight near the front and effectively improves the accuracy of a throw. Since the 1930s, brass barrels have been almost exclusively used, but in recent years some top players have switched to tungsten. Almost twice as dense as brass, tungsten barrels are considerably thinner than those made from brass, and so allow for an easier grouping of the darts on the board ("three in a bed").

Turkey feathers are the material of choice for flights, but because the birds are now raised in confined quarters, pros claim the feathers aren't as strong as before. To prevent damage to a flight when another dart passes by it on the board, any alternative material must be flexible. Polyester flights fit this requirement and have become popular, both for this reason and because they are reasonably priced.

Most dart makers use plastic for the shaft. Titanium is gaining in popularity among the pros, but its cost is prohibitive for most others. Besides being durable, titanium is so strong that the shaft can be significantly thinner than that required for a plastic model, thereby facilitating close passage by neighboring darts.

The Science

As common as darts are around the world, few studies have tackled the physics behind a bull's-eye. A lack of consistency in the way people play contributes to the difficulty scientists encounter when analyzing the game.

Unicorn Products, Ltd., a London dart maker and sponsor of many of today's championship games, years ago asked a British government laboratory for help in designing the perfect dart. The conclusion: There isn't such a thing. "They said there was too much variability in the throws and the trajectories people use," says Stanley Lowry of Unicorn. "We've found the same thing here in our research department. We've built throwing machines to test darts, but we didn't find them terribly useful because while we can reproduce an average throw, we've never found a player who has an average throw."

About all that can be said is that when a dart is thrown, gravity attempts to drag the point downward, but the flight invokes air resistance that forces the nose back up again **(see Figure 6–2)**. A typical dart travels about 40 mph (58.7 ft/sec), so in tournament play it takes about 0.14 second to travel the eight feet to the board. (Actually, the distance is 7 feet, 9¼ inches. This oddball distance is the result of a compromise made about fifteen years ago between the British—who used eight feet—and the Americans, who used seven and a half feet.)

Although there are almost as many ways to throw a dart as there are dart players, the pros do show considerable consistency in their stance, throw, and grip.

The Stance

The only body part that should move when a dart is thrown is the arm. Stability is important. That's really why beer and darts go hand-in-hand: A large beer belly lowers the body's center of gravity and discourages sway. The bigger the belly, the better the anchor, you might say.

Big belly or no, the feet should be flat on the ground and pointed

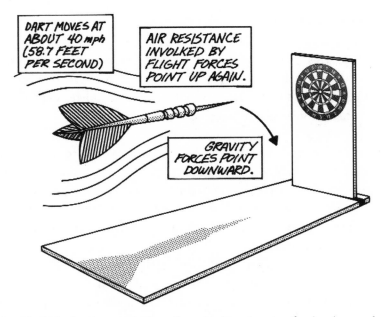

6-2 *The Path of a Dart. As the force of gravity drags the point of a dart downward, the feathers invoke air resistance, which brings the nose back up again.*

toward the target. The key is to be well-balanced, which for most people means having about 60 percent of their weight on the right foot.

The Throw

Both eyes should be kept open. The four F's that govern dart throwing are: firm, fast, flat trajectory, and a smooth follow-through.

Sandy Reitan-Green, considered the American queen of darts, says "Darts is a game played with two things—the wrist and the mind. You have to hold the dart out in front of you, so that you can keep that hand-eye coordination going, and you shoot from the wrist."

The Grip

For a player just starting out, who hasn't settled into a grip of his or her own making, the best way to hold the dart is with three fingers and the thumb: the index and middle fingers above the dart, and the ring finger and thumb below.

Mental Practice

Many athletes find that practicing their game mentally improves their success on the field. (See Chapter 2: Basketball, for more on visualization.) Although a darter can hardly be called an athlete, some players still benefit from using this technique.

Harvey Wichman and Paul Lizotte, of Claremont McKenna College, examined the effect of mental practice on dart games. Their conclusion: It can produce a significant increase in accuracy, but almost exclusively for participants with an "internal locus of control." By internal locus of control they mean people who interpret outcomes as a consequence of their own actions, rather than from outside influences, such as chance or fate.

Participants in the study sat comfortably, with their eyes closed and their hands in their laps. Extensive visualization processes ensued, including throwing the darts at a target, feeling the darts in their hands, and imagining the sound the darts made when hitting a board. They also mentally corrected any imagined misses. The research team found that significant improvements resulted from mentally practicing for a total of only 24 minutes (two 3-minute sessions a day for four days).

One has to ask if mental practice is so often effective, could it help an investor amass a personal fortune? (Come to think of it, there is a book called *Think and Grow Rich*.) Maybe, but if thinking won't do it, throwing a dart might. In 1967, *Forbes* magazine put together a random portfolio using dart throws. The original selection included twenty-eight stocks, but by 1984 acquisitions and mergers had shrunk the list down to fifteen companies and the hypothetical fund was put to rest. During its lifetime, however, the portfolio beat the Dow Jones Industrial by more than 10 to 1.

Alcohol and Darts

Teetotaling dart players: is this an oxymoron?

The history of darts is steeped in brown ale and kindred spirits, but such a state may be going the way of the three-martini lunch. In San

Diego, for example, Danny Ledcke opened a nonalcoholic dart parlor behind his dart supply store. Although supported by the 440-member Darting Association, not everyone is happy about it. Some teams refuse to play there, saying it is too much like a cake and ice cream social. Ledcke responds that "Darts has always been a pub sport. Well, I'm saying maybe it's time for a change."

Most dart players would argue with him because they believe a few beers help them relax and hence play a better game. Studies have shown, however, that alcohol consumption probably doesn't actually reduce anxiety in the pharmaceutical sense, per se, but rather reduces "self-awareness." Even more specifically, it inhibits negative self-reactions.

This theory in turn gives credence to the idea that learning may be "state-dependent." In other words, a task or skill learned while under the influence may not be easily duplicated when the player is sober. If a player is less self-aware when "feeling happy," and learns to play under these conditions, when sober he may be more self-conscience and consequently think too hard. Thus, this theory could explain why darters who routinely drink while practicing don't do as well at tournament games if they go "on the wagon."

Can bad company at the pub drive a person to drink? Apparently so. Two studies done under psychologist R. Lorraine Collins at the Research Institute on Alcoholism are relevant to this question. She reports that a person will vary the amount of alcohol consumed depending on whether or not a drinking partner is sociable. When with a sociable partner, a person will tend to match the drinking rate exhibited by the other person. However, when with an unsociable partner, a person will tend to drink heavily, regardless of how much the other is drinking. The same researchers found that people's perception of a heavy drinker is directly related to the drinker's social status. A laborer drinking three beers is perceived to be a heavy drinker; a medical resident drinking the same amount is seen as a light drinker. Sounds like darters should wear a suit to the pub—or maybe medical whites.

Chapter 7

Diving the Depths

A World Beyond

"Wow! I can breathe under water. This stuff really works!"
—*Jerry Martin, Quoting a typical reaction of beginning scuba divers*

It's hard to capture in words the sensation a diver feels as he roams a coral reef, supported by warm water teeming with life forms more alien than any H.G. Wells could have imagined. A kaleidoscope of colors dazzles the eyes; a friendly parrot fish noses up to say hello.

But just as an astronaut can't land on the moon without preparation, a diver must also adhere to certain rules to ensure a safe and pleasant journey underwater. These rules, along with practical experience, are taught at diver certification classes.

Having a "C" card allows a diver to rent equipment almost anywhere in the world, and usually is necessary before operators will fill a diver's air tanks. The payoff comes when a diver comfortably explores a coral reef or investigates an ancient shipwreck—opening a world unparalleled in beauty and high drama.

The following information naturally includes some topics covered in a certification course, but a person armed with this knowledge is still not qualified to dive. Such qualification can only come from successfully completing a certified diving course.

Pressure

Two types of pressure manifestations are important to a diver: atmospheric pressure and water pressure. Atmospheric pressure, as its name implies, results from the weight of the atmosphere pressing down on the earth's surface. This weight produces a force of about 14.7 pounds per square inch (psi), so pressure of this amount is commonly called one atmosphere. Although 14.7 psi might not sound like much, at sea level the cumulative pressure on the 15 to 20 square feet of surface area on a human body mounts to an astounding 37,000 pounds. Because our bodies feel this pressure uniformly all the time, we don't particularly notice it. We would notice, however, if it suddenly disappeared!

Water weighs about 64 pounds per cubic foot and also generates pressure. As the depth of the water increases, so does the pressure, because the amount of weight bearing down at that point also increases. Water pressure increases at a rate of 0.445 psi per foot of depth in saltwater, and 0.432 psi per foot in fresh water (saltwater is heavier than fresh water; 64 and 62.4 pounds per cubic foot, respectively). Hence, 33 feet of saltwater generates 14.7 psi, or one atmosphere. Two atmospheres occur at 66 feet, three at 99 feet, and so on.

Since pressure gauges are normally set to read zero at sea level, a diver calculating pounds per square inch "absolute" (psia) pressure must add 14.7 psi to the pounds per square inch "gauge" (psig) pressure to obtain the total pressure bearing down on him **(see Table 7-1)**. Calculations concerning a dive must use absolute pressure, not gauge pressure.

Table 7-1
Pressure Increase by Feet of Depth

ATMOSPHERES	DEPTH IN SALTWATER (FEET)	GAUGE PRESSURE (PSIG)	ABSOLUTE PRESSURE (PSIA)
1	Surface	0	14.7
2	33	14.7	29.4
3	66	29.4	44.1
4	99	44.1	58.8
5	132	58.8	73.5
6	165	73.5	88.2
7	198	88.2	102.9

By its nature, pressure exerts force evenly on any object, regardless of the object's shape. However, the molecular structure (be it solid, liquid, or gas) can greatly influence the reaction to that force. Liquids and solids, for the most part, are incompressible. Gases, on the other hand, compress easily and obey Boyle's law. This law states that, given a constant temperature and change in pressure, the density of a gas will vary directly with the change in pressure, and the volume will change inversely. To a

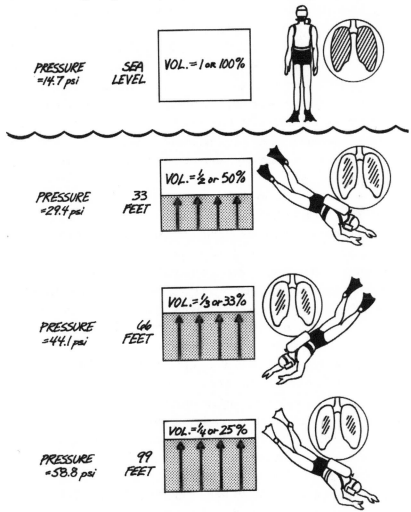

PRESSURE =14.7 psi   **SEA LEVEL**   VOL.=1 or 100%

PRESSURE =29.4 psi   33 FEET   VOL.=½ or 50%

PRESSURE =44.1 psi   66 FEET   VOL.=⅓ or 33%

PRESSURE =58.8 psi   99 FEET   VOL.=¼ or 25%

7-1 *Boyle's Law. Given a constant temperature and change in pressure, the density of a gas will vary directly with the change in pressure, and the volume will change inversely. To a diver, this means that with each doubling of pressure, the gas' density likewise doubles, but its volume decreases by 50 percent.*

diver, this means that if the pressure doubles, density of the gas likewise doubles, but the volume decreases by 50 percent **(see Figure 7-1)**.

Pressure alone doesn't ordinarily cause problems, but pockets of unequal pressure attempting to achieve equilibrium can. Because liquids and solids make up most of the human body, it is, up to a point, impervious to pressure. Not so the body's air cavities. The lungs, sinuses, and middle ear all have air cavities that, lacking equalized pressure, will collapse until equilibrium is reached. A properly functioning regulator prevents injury from occurring to these cells by delivering air that is equal in pressure to the surrounding, or ambient, water pressure. The lungs distribute this pressurized air throughout all areas of the body, including the sinuses and ears, thereby equalizing the pressure within. A diver breathing regularly, therefore, should experience no injury to these fragile membranes.

A blocked passageway, however—say, the eustachian tube of the middle ear—makes equilibrium impossible and the resulting pressure differential can lead at a minimum to pain, and at an extreme to permanent damage to the eardrum and surrounding blood vessels. Similarly, a head cold can prevent the sinuses from equalizing, so a diver having this condition should not dive that day. Divers suffering from allergies that block the sinuses should also avoid diving until the condition clears.

An equally important consequence of Boyle's law is that the volume of air in the lungs decreases by 50 percent for each atmosphere a diver descends. In other words, the volume of air needed to fill the lungs doubles for each 33 feet of depth. For descent, this simply means that the diver consumes more air per minute than on the surface. Where problems arise is on the ascent. Here, the air rapidly expands as the diver travels upward. One lungful at 66 feet of depth is equal to three lungfuls at the surface. If the diver doesn't expel this extra air, serious consequences can result, ranging from burst lungs to air embolisms. With the latter, air bubbles are forced from the lungs into the surrounding blood vessels, where they can quickly travel to the heart or brain. Not much margin for error exists: if the lungs are fully expanded, rising only four feet can put the diver at grave risk. Cardinal rules in scuba, therefore, are to always breathe normally and regularly, and to ascend slowly.

Air pockets on the outside of the body are also subject to pressure differentials, or "squeeze," and can lead to discomfort, more so than danger, during a descent. Unequal air pressure in a face mask, for example, causes eye squeeze, which, if not equalized, can cause tiny veins in the eye to rupture. (Simply exhaling gently through the nose should take care of this problem.) Suit squeeze can pinch the skin when air bubbles are present in a dive suit—a much more common occurrence with dry suits than with wet suits. Welts and ridges mark the skin where this occurs.

Air Supply

Scuba (which stands for self-contained underwater breathing apparatus) can be either open-circuit, with a diver exhaling air into the surrounding water, or closed-circuit, with the exhaled air being filtered and recirculated. Although closed-circuit scuba is still used in the military, sports diving always uses open-circuit systems.

Alveolar exhange is the transposition of oxygen from air into the bloodstream and simultaneous removal of carbon dioxide from the lungs. Essentially, five steps occur in this process:

- Oxygen is breathed into the lungs, where it enters the alveoli (tiny air sacs) and diffuses into the blood vessels surrounding the alveoli.
- The pulmonary veins transport this oxygen-rich blood to the heart.
- The aorta pumps this blood throughout the body.
- As the blood passes through tissue capillaries, the oxygen is extracted to fuel the body's need for energy. (See Chapter 8: Football, "The Trainer as Chemist.") Carbon dioxide is a byproduct of this "cellular respiration."
- The carbon dioxide is carried back to the heart and then to the lungs, where it diffuses into the alveoli and is expelled by breathing.

At rest, we inhale slightly less than one pint of air per minute; heavy exercise or breathing can increase this volume tenfold. A factor known as RMV (respiratory minute volume) measures the total volume of air needed for oxygen intake and carbon dioxide expulsion. Underwater, this volume varies from one pint per minute (at rest) to 50 pints per minute (seeing a shark and—not recommended—swimming frantically away).

If it weren't for the need to expel carbon dioxide, a diver's consumption rate of air would be the same regardless of depth. Gas volumes decrease with depth, but the density of the oxygen molecules within the gas increases proportionately; hence, if oxygen consumption were the only criterion for total air consumption, the rate would remain constant, however deep the dive. But the expulsion of carbon dioxide depends entirely on the total volume of gas inhaled and exhaled, and that amount is the same whether a diver is at the surface or 500 feet deep. Because the volume of air decreases as a diver descends, the demand for more air increases proportionately—doubling at 33 feet, tripling at 66 feet, and so on. Thus, a standard 71.2-cubic-foot tank, fully charged, may give a diver 90 minutes of air at sea level, but only 45 minutes at one atmosphere (33 feet), or 30 minutes at two atmospheres (66 feet).

Two other important laws governing divers are Dalton's law and Henry's law. Dalton's law of partial pressures states that in a mixture of gases, the pressure each gas exerts is proportional to its percentage of the total mixture. The mixture of air on earth, and therefore in compressed air, is about 78 percent nitrogen, 21 percent oxygen, and 1 percent other inert gases. Thus, according to Dalton, oxygen accounts for about one-fifth the total pressure in a tank, and nitrogen about four-fifths. These fractions are called partial pressures. Henry's law of solubility explains the relationship between gases and liquids, and consequently determines how much of each gas a diver's bloodstream absorbs. The consequences of this law cause divers the most grief.

Specifically, this law states that the total amount (concentration) of gas soluble in a liquid is proportional to the partial pressure of that gas. As a body descends, it absorbs more nitrogen, the chief constituent of air, than it may be able to safely pass off through the alveolar exchange process. Pressure causes the nitrogen to go into solution, and the body stores it in muscles and tissues, especially in fatty tissues. In a normal dive with a slow ascent, regular breathing coupled with a gradual reduction of pressure allows this gas to be safely transported in solution back into the blood and hence to the lungs for elimination.

If pressure decreases too quickly during a rapid ascent, though, the nitrogen comes out of solution and bubbles form, leading to potentially serious problems. Opening a champagne bottle presents a visual display of this phenomenon. Champagne's effervescence comes from carbon dioxide dissolved into it under high pressure. If the bottle is opened slowly, the pressure differences between the inside and outside of the bottle steadily equalize, and the cork makes a satisfactory pop as it exits the bottle. In this case, the carbon dioxide has stayed in solution. If, however, the bottle is opened too fast, the tension holding the carbon dioxide in solution breaks, and the gas quickly exits the bottle in the form of bubbles, taking some of the wine with it. (If it's a bottle of Dom Perignon, tears also flow.)

The same phenomenon happens if a diver ascends too quickly, only the gas is nitrogen, and there isn't any easy escape route. Consequently, the bubbles lodge in constricted areas of the circulatory system—the joints, muscles, and spinal cord, for example.

Properly called decompression sickness (DCS), this reaction is also knows as the Grecian bends or bends. The term originated in the late nineteenth century to describe a posture or walk, often considered fashionable at the time, in which the body was bent forward from the waist. When the Brooklyn Bridge in New York was under construction, workers in the closed, watertight tunnels would suffer pain that caused them to "bend over like a woman affecting the Grecian bends." Since that time, the term has been used to describe decompression sickness. Strictly speaking, today the term bends should be used only in reference to the painful form of DCS. Other symptoms are rashes and fatigue, both indicating the presence of bubbles in the system. If bubbles locate in the central nervous system, the diver can experience dizziness, numbness, blurred vision, and hearing defects. These latter symptoms, which can show up even after a perfectly normal dive, indicate a need to see a doctor, because some part of the nervous system is being deprived of its blood supply. Although death caused by DCS is exceedingly rare (only five of the 1,083 sport scuba diving fatalities reported from 1975 to

1984), permanent neurological disabilities can result from nonfatal DCS. Symptoms can occur minutes or hours after diving.

Treatment for serious cases of decompression sickness includes the use of decompression chambers, technically called hyperbaric chambers. The victim is "recompressed," often at depths of 165 feet or thereabouts, until the nitrogen bubbles go back into solution. Pressure is then gradually reduced, allowing the nitrogen to leave the body in a normal process—through the blood and lungs. Pure oxygen is generally administered in the process, but not until chamber pressure is equivalent to a depth of 60 feet or less. At greater pressures, oxygen toxicity can occur, leading to convulsions.

Fortunately for divers, the availability of hyperbaric chambers has greatly increased in recent years. The Diving Alert Network, headquartered at Duke University Medical Canter, provides help both in diagnosis and in locating the closest hyperbaric chamber. For emergencies, the telephone number is (919) 684-8111. A nonprofit organization, the network also offers medical insurance at a reasonable price that covers recompression chamber and air ambulance costs for diving-related accidents. Transportation to a facility can be expensive, because it must be either in a plane flying no more that 1,000 feet above the original ground level or in a plane that can maintain sea-level cabin pressure; otherwise, a decrease in barometric pressure could cause the bubbles to expand.

The body can store a certain amount of nitrogen without having a problem with bubbles forming. Depending on the time and depth of the dive, however, it may be necessary to make decompression stops during the ascent, which allow time for desaturation of the blood and body tissues.

The U.S. Navy developed decompression tables that for thirty years have been widely used by divers. These tables show the length and number of stops needed for dives of a specific time and depth. Stops are generally not required for very short or shallow dives (although some professionals still advise stopping at 10 feet for a few minutes on all dives). **Table 7–2** summarized the Navy's "no-decompression limits"; that is, those dives that can be made without decompression stops. "Bottom time in minutes" is somewhat a misnomer because it actually the total elapsed time after leaving the surface and before beginning the ascent, not the time actually spent on the bottom. Many diving classes use tables more conservative than the Navy's; that is, they allow less bottom time in minutes for each depth category, and the "no-limit bottom time" may end at a shallower depth (26 feet, for example). Being conservative makes good sense, because sports divers are often not as physically fit as Navy divers, nor as practiced.

Table 7–2
No-Decompression Limits

DEPTH (FEET)*	BOTTOM TIME (MINUTES)
LESS THAN 33	NO LIMIT
35	310
40	200
50	100
60	60
70	50
80	40
90	30
100	25
110	20
120	15
130	10

Sports divers normally shouldn't exceed 60 to 70 feet, with an absolute maximum of 100 feet.

Proper use of the tables is taught at diver-certification classes, and because no diver should pursue this activity without a certificate, details are omitted here. It suffices to say that if more than one dive is made within 12 hours, the tables become considerably more complex. They are also inappropriate for mountain lake diving unless adjusted for altitude. The tables include an ascent time, based on an ascent speed of 60 feet per minute (one foot per second) that a diver must maintain. (Some diving schools recommend an even slower ascent rate, such as 30 to 40 feet per minute, which, because more time is spent getting to the surface, allows less time "at the bottom.")

Rarely, divers using the tables exactly as instructed still develop the bends. So many variables exist that can affect individual dives that neither the Navy not the Professional Association of Diving Instructors (PADI—whose members train about 70 percent of the divers in North America) can completely guarantee the safe application of the tables. PADI recently released its own tables that the association considers more applicable to sports diving. The new tables use a 120-minute "critical tissue half-time"; that is, the time required for the gas pressure in a tissue to rise or fall halfway to the gas pressure outside the tissue. For multiple dives, this change effectively shortens the diving time for early dives and gives longer times for later dives.

Certain factors seem to increase a diver's susceptibility to DCS. A female, for example, is more susceptible because of her body's higher fat content, as fat tissues absorb nitrogen faster than other types of tissue. (On the flip side, females generally have smaller lung capacities which, because they use less air, allow them to get more time from a tank of air.) How hydrated a diver is also makes a difference; a well-hydrated body is less susceptible. Other factors having an influence are water temperature and the use of salicylates (aspirin).

Sometimes unknown factors protect a diver from developing DCS. Hawaiian diver-fisherman routinely make deep dives without using decompression stops. Apparently, some of them may have genetically evolved in a special way. Not all of them, however. Jerry Martin, the owner and general manager of two Northwest Divers shops in Tacoma, Washington, has treated many Hawaiian divers for DCS. He says that while stationed at Pearl Harbor at a diving station, he saw extensive use of the decompression tank, often for divers who believed they were immune to DCS but who turned out not to be. Still, it would be interesting to study those who are immune and determine how they got that way.

Another possible water hazard: drunk drivers . . .er, rather, drunk divers. An interesting consequence of nitrogen absorption is nitrogen narcosis, described by Jacques Cousteau as "rapture of the deep." This effect is believed to result from a process similar to that induced by nitrous oxide (laughing gas). The mental effects of each 50 feet of descent are approximately equal to that experience from imbibing one dry martini, so this phenomenon used to be known as Martini's law. Today's instructors avoid this term, both because of a change in attitude concerning drinking, and because it is so vague—after all, how much vermouth makes a martini dry?

Susceptibility to nitrogen narcosis varies greatly among individuals, but each diver must be alert for its effects. A popular story has circulated for ages among divers: A professional deep-sea diver was at about 250 feet, connected to his tender by a voice-communication system. Suddenly, the diver started rambling incoherently, and the crew couldn't understand him. Finally, they made out the following: "This blankety-blank air hose is getting in the way something fierce, but not to worry—I almost have it cut off." Needless to say, the crew raised the man topside in short order. (Not too quickly, obviously, or he would have gotten the bends.)

More seriously, alcohol and diving make a terrible combination. On Martin's expeditions, alcohol is prohibited for six hours before and after a dive. "Once they pull the tab, they can't dive anymore that day." His rationale: alcohol or drug use changes the physiological functions of the body and can cause serious problems, such as the bends—not to mention that a diver should avoid using anything that could possibly cause disorientation.

Martin also advises that divers older than 40 be more conservative in using the diving tables. "For some reason, circulatory and physiological changes occur and the body doesn't release nitrogen as fast, so older divers are more susceptible to the bends." He also recommends that all divers stop at 15 feet for three minutes to decompress, regardless of the depth and time of the dive.

The Water Environment

Water covers about 70 percent of the earth's surface, so man's quest to understand this alien environment is understandable. There's so much of it, that if a major catastrophe were to level all of the earth's surface features, we would all be under two miles of water.

Various environmental conditions determine how well we navigate through water, and these vary depending on where the dive is taking place. Water's buoyancy, temperature, and viscosity all play a part in affecting the ease of a dive.

The principles governing buoyancy explain why a boat sitting on top of the water doesn't sink, but a two-ounce piece of lead thrown overboard by the fisherman immediately drops to the bottom. It's all a matter of the density of the materials.

Density expresses an object's weight or mass per unit volume, such as "three pounds per cubic inch." Materials have various weights because of the varied density of particles within them. Balsa wood, for example, has considerably fewer particles per unit volume than does lead; hence, it is less dense and consequently lighter. Relative density is expressed in terms of specific gravity, with pure water having a standard value of 1.0. Other materials are compared to this standard. Mercury, for example, has a specific gravity of 13.6; hence, it weighs 13.6 times more than water per unit volume.

Saltwater on average has a specific gravity of 1.03. If the salt content is very high, as in the Great Salt Lake, the specific gravity is correspondingly higher. A human body, which is about 70 percent water, generally has an overall specific gravity slightly less than 1.0. Most people, therefore, tend to float in salt water, a condition described as positive buoyancy. If they tend to stay at the same depth, they have neutral buoyancy, while "sinkers" have negative buoyancy.

Whether an object floats or sinks is governed by Archimedes' principle: A body floating in a fluid displaces a weight of fluid equal to its own weight. In other words, if the body weighs less than the amount of fluid it displaces, it floats.

A diver uses two pieces of equipment to help control buoyancy. Weight belts, with quick-release safety catches, allow a diver to add one, two, three, or five pounds of weight, singly or in combination. The diver attaches these weights before a dive, striving for neutral buoyancy. After a dive has begun, buoyancy control devices (BCDs) compensate for changes that occur during the dive itself. Although pressure doesn't alter the body's buoyancy a noticeable amount, overall changes do result from the emptying air tank, from compression of gas spaces in clothing and wet suits, and from compression of the BCDs themselves. These handy devices can be inflated manually for directly from the scuba tank.

Temperature also affects a diver in various ways. Because water is considerably more efficient at conducting heat than air (by about four times), water even a few degrees colder than 98.6° F can expose a diver to chilling. Wet suits make a big difference; even thin ones can lessen the heat loss by as much as 80 percent (but only for the skin they are actually covering). Cold water also speeds up the body's metabolism, which can lead to fatigue, and can reduce a diver's ability to perform both mentally and physically.

Various temperature zones, called thermoclines, are often encountered even on shallow dives. Water at the surface may be 70° F, but can the drop as much as 30 to 40° at the bottom, even for dives of less than 100 feet.

The viscosity of water makes it harder to move through than air. Drag resistance is the primary component influencing viscosity, and in water it increases approximately as the square of the velocity. Therefore, a diver who starts to swim twice as fast will encounter four times the drag resistance. Fins help by increasing a diver's mobility by as much as five times (as compared with bare feet). Scuba "sleds" have also gained in popularity as an aid to locomotion. One particular model doesn't even require batteries—it runs off the diver's air supply. The "engine exhaust" is then used for breathing. In that swimming increases a diver's need for air by about three times over a motionless state, sleds can easily help extend the time spent and distance traveled underwater.

Diving Computers

High tech hits the high seas as more divers use sophisticated computers to keep track of how much diving time remains. A diver straps this calculating marvel, pioneered by Orca Industries, to his wrist or carries it in an instrument console. The computers make up for a major deficiency of the dive tables; that is, adjusting for a diver's motion through various depths. Thus, the tables do not "give credit" for time spent at shallower levels, and strict use of them can cut a dive short. The computer, on the other hand, keeps track of total dive time, water temperature, depth, air supply, and nitrogen absorption—and updates the information every three seconds. (Still, a diver should always know the tables as a backup measure.)

Some divers still believe the device to be nothing but an expensive toy. Typical reactions range from "Now that I've tried one, I couldn't live without one," to "I don't trust this newfangled technology and wouldn't be caught in a swimming pool with one."

Computers are especially valuable for multiple dive situations. On tropical vacations, for example, when two or three dives are made each day for numerous days it becomes very difficult to keep tract of nitrogen buildup. Computers take the guesswork out and allow divers to spend their time doing what they love the most—diving.

Chapter 8
Football

Flying Pigskin

"Luck is what happens when preparation meets opportunity."
            —*Darrell Royal, Former coach, Texas University Longhorns*

The town of Ada, Ohio, will never qualify as an American hot spot. As resident Peggy Price puts it, "The last exciting thing that happened in Ada was back in '78, when they put in a new sewer line." Nevertheless, the people of this small burg can take credit for providing plenty of excitement elsewhere: they make more than a million footballs for the Wilson Company each year, including those used in NFL games.

Since its inception as an organized game in the United States, people have associated football with pigskin. Strange, because the balls have always been made from cowhide. This misnomer probably arose from historical references to *futballe*, an English game played in the twelfth century that used inflated pig bladders as balls.

But cows (and the Wilson Company) had better watch out—competition is lurking in the wings. Rawlings Sporting Goods Company, famous for baseballs, has recently introduced a football made of a composite material that is reportedly better than current NFL footballs in compressibility, fatigue, and water resistance. Called the Kevlar 29 ST-5 football, it absorbs less moisture and so allows for more accurate passing and kicking. Collegiate teams in particular like and are ordering the ball.

Whatever the material, a football inspires fans and players alike as it makes it's way down the field, albeit slowly at times. The most exciting moments happen when the ball spirals a great distance from either an expert punt or pass.

The Mechanics of a Spiral

Other than having a pointed nose, a football doesn't seem particularly aerodynamic. It's certainly true that one thrown without spin will rapidly tumble from the sky. Ah, but add spin and suddenly the ball

8-1   *Spin on a Forward Pass. The spinning put on pass gives its flight what physicists call gyroscopic stability.*

becomes an aerodynamic marvel, capable of carving out a perfect curve over the field. How can the addition of such a minor element change a football from a dud to a "field bomb"? By endowing the ball with what physicists call gyroscopic stability **(see Figure 8-1)**. An object rapidly spinning tends to keep spinning until opposing forces cause it to stop. For an object in the air, the spinning motion imparts a stability to the flight that would otherwise not exist. Quarterbacks Johnny Unitas and Dan Marino certainly understood this principle, and as a result achieved great fame for their elegant spiral passes.

Both obviously were skilled at foiling the forces trying to bring the ball down, the strongest of these being drag, which results from air resistance. Compared with a baseball, tennis ball, or even a Frisbee, a football presents many more faces of various shapes to the air; hence, it can have a much less predictable flight. Nose-first, its surface area is about 0.25 square feet. Broadside, it almost doubles to 0.41 square feet. Drag forces accordingly vary from 0.15 pound to 1.50 pounds, the latter exceeding what a football weighs.

This doesn't mean a ball should go "dead into the wind," however. It must make a proper angle of attack. A ball's trajectory is the line described by its center of mass. How much the front of an object is offset from this line defines its angle of attack. The magnitude of this angle determines the amount of lift generated. For a football going nose-to-the-wind, a 10-degree angle is best. More than that will generate excessive lift, and rather than describing a gentle curve, the ball will swoosh upward rapidly and come back down the same way. For a long field pass, such a trajectory will probably not give the ball enough hang time (the time the ball is in the air) for a receiver to get down to the field to catch it.

Fast receivers sprint down the field at about 18 mph. A 50-yard pass, therefore, needs to be in the air about 6.0 seconds. Add the second or two it takes the receiver to fight off a block, and clearly the longer the ball is in the air the better. Of course, if he's lucky, a receiver is also aided by the additional time a passer is allowed by his linemen while getting into a position to throw.

Whether passing or kicking, a player must decide if he wants a long hang time or distance down the field—he can't maximize both. The hang time depends on the initial velocity of the ball and on how high an arc is made as a result of the launch angle. The higher the arc, the less horizontal distance achieved **(see Figure 8-2)**.

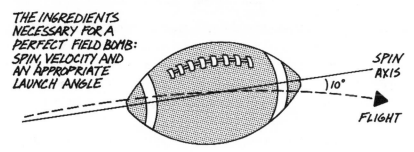

8-2 *A Perfect Field Bomb. The time the ball is in the air (hang time) depends on the initial velocity of the ball and on how high an arc is made as a result of the launch angle.*

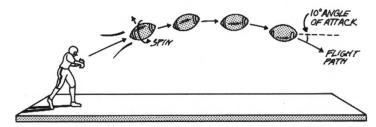

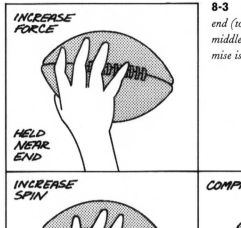

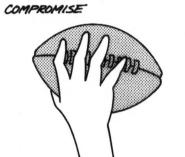

8-3   *Grips. Holding the ball near the end (top) increases force. Holding it in the middle increases spin. The usual compromise is in between.*

The ball's initial velocity also influences its trajectory, because more speed means less drag. A perfect range for a field bomb is between 40 to 45 mph. (Passes made by Bronco John Elway may seem at times to exceed this speed, perhaps because of the improbable positions he puts himself in to throw them. Watching him play, it becomes obvious why he's known as having a "gun for an arm.")

Even for players lacking Elway's power, it's relatively easy to put spin on a forward pass, although the grip is somewhat awkward for beginners. To generate spin, the hand must be near the ball's center of gravity; that is, near the middle. Conversely, to generate force, the hand needs to be as far back on the ball as possible. A player compromises these two needs and grips the ball as far back as he can while maintaining control of the ball **(see Figure 8–3)**. He'll know if he hasn't launched it with enough spin—wobble sets in almost immediately. A good pass generally spins at about 600 revolutions per minute. (Then again, both Billy Kilmer and Joe Kapp—highly successful quarterbacks—were known for their "wobbly" passes. Somehow, they still got the job done.)

Kicking a ball presents more challenges in some respects than does passing. Whether punting or place kicking, spin is still needed to ensure a stable flight. Punters achieve this (although only about 60 percent of the time) by simultaneously hitting the bottom of the ball and angling their leg from one side to the other. Concentration is essential: ask Clint Wager, who was a punter for the old Chicago Cardinals. Practicing one day, he became distracted and kicked himself in the head, hard enough to inflict a fractured jaw. Although gymnasts may be impressed with Wager's flexibility, this is not the way to get a good angle on the ball.

A placekicker can't kick the way a punter does because the ball rests on a tee. His task is perhaps the most challenging of all: the ball must be hit enough off center and with enough force to make it tumble end over end (for all but the shortest field goals or point-after attempts). The axis of rotation is not through the center of the ball, but nonetheless does exist, giving the ball some gyroscopic stability.

Peter Brancazio, cited earlier for his studies in basketball, has also studied the physics of football kicking. He attempted to calculate the appropriate launch angle for kicks resulting in maximum distance, hang time, or both. He determined that successful punts are launched at as low as 50 degrees to gain distance and as high as 70 degrees to gain hang time. Kickoffs are generally launched at 45 degrees to maximize their distance down the field. The successful long, high kicks were launched at between 55 and 60 degrees.

The successful completion of a pass or punt often requires that at least one member of the team advance down the field fast. Chemistry and biomechanics now come into play.

The Trainer as Chemist

Today's coaches know much more than just how to pick out and train good players. Advances in sports physiology make it imperative that they also know about chemistry and physics, at least as the subjects relate to human performance.

Muscle contractions, the basis of all movement, are fueled by an energy production system more awesome and complex than any modern power plant designed by man. Without thought, our systems differentiate the need for long-term energy production (endurance) and the need for short, intense bursts of energy (strength). Different chemical reactions come into play (aerobic versus anaerobic), and different muscle fibers are stressed (slow-twitch versus fast-twitch).

Picture a wide receiver about to receive a pass. Before he can even move, his muscles receive a command from his central nervous system, which relays this command to individual muscles via individual nerve impulses. One impulse can trigger from five to several hundred muscle fibers simultaneously. Each fiber is actually a single, elongated cell, microscopically thin and usually a couple of inches long (but sometimes as long as the muscle group it resides in). When the impulse arrives at the junction of the nerve and muscle, chemical transmitters spark a change in voltage across the muscle membrane, which induces a release of calcium.

This calcium then enters the gap between filaments of muscle fiber, triggering a complex chemical reaction that includes the breakdown of ATP (adenosine triphosphate), a molecule consisting of three phosphate groups. As the chemical bond holding the ATP molecule intact is broken, energy is released, fueling the muscle contraction. Thousands of these reactions occur as the receiver races down the field.

After each contraction, the ATP molecule must be quickly "reassembled" for the next reaction. It is at this point that, depending on the intensity and type of activity, our bodies employ one of four possible processes for energy production. Two of these are aerobic, meaning they use oxygen, and two are anaerobic, meaning they do not.

Now imagine our wide receiver catching a long bomb. Chances are, he won't inhale during this run. In the absence of oxygen, his body can reconstruct the ATP molecule using a combination of phosphocreatin (PC) or glucose (converted from glycogen in a process called glycolysis). However, pyruvic acid forms as a by-product of these chemical reactions, which, without oxygen (anaerobic glycolysis), converts into lactic acid. An accumulation of this acid leads to muscle fatigue. If oxygen is present, however (aerobic glycolysis), pyruvic acid converts to water and carbon dioxide, which his body will easily discard.

Our wide receiver might also make use of aerobic fat-metabolism. Here, oxygen and fat combine in a reaction that releases energy, carbon dioxide, and water, but not harmful waste products such as pyruvic acid.

Endurance activities favor the aerobic process, because it can continue indefinitely, so long as an adequate supply of glycogen or fat exists. Anaerobic processes, on the other hand, only provide energy for brief, intense spurts; 30 seconds for an ATP-PC process, 2 minutes for the anaerobic glycolysis process. Energy for fast sprints, such as a five-second run in football, is provided almost entirely by the anaerobic process. One famous run by a player who probably ran long enough to induce the aerobic process is that by Snooks Dowd, who played for Lehigh University in the early 1900s. Dowd inadvertently ran the wrong way down the field, clear to his own goal line. Realizing his mistake, he then ran the right way—managed to get past all of the tackles—and made a touchdown.

Key to the aerobic process are minuscule structures in the muscle cells called mitochondria, which consume oxygen, break down carbohydrates and fats, and produce ATP. Endurance training can increase the number of mitochondria by as much as 100 percent (with a resulting 400 percent increase in endurance). Strength training, however, has virtually no effect on the number of these energy generators.

Mitochondria play a major role in what is mistakenly called oxygen debt. After running 40 yards down the field, a player's heart often continues to beat rapidly, and he breathes hard. Believing this sensation to be the result of oxygen deprivation, chances are we'll see him sucking up oxygen at the sidelines. This response has erroneously been attributed to a buildup of lactic acid, supposedly as a result of oxygen deprivation. Studies have shown, however, that internal heat is actually the culprit. The same chemical reaction that produces energy for muscle contractions produces heat as a byproduct. This heat invokes an increased need for oxygen by the mitochondria, which have stopped producing energy (ATP) but still consume oxygen. Physiologist George A. Brooks, of the University of California at Berkeley, believes that "elevated post-exercise oxygen consumption" would better describe the condition than oxygen debt.

Thus, in that oxygen deprivation isn't the real problem, at least not directly, it is unlikely that supplemental oxygen is helping the player physically in this regard. It might seem so to him, however, just because the inhaled air is cooler than the ambient air temperature—and it might clear his head a bit, getting him ready for the next rush.

The Biomechanics of a Rush

Former Bronco running back Blake Ezor laughed the first time the coach made him run along a Denver track with a parachute billowing behind him—but not for long. Using the Speed Chute in training for a couple of weeks enabled him to lower his time in the 40-yard dash by 0.04 seconds. Although Ezor considered the chute a "real drag," it paid off for him. Such is the wonder of biomechanics, the science of the human body in motion.

In the early seventies, most football teams didn't even own weight-lifting equipment. Today, they routinely spend millions of dollars on various equipment designed to give their players an edge in strength, speed, and agility. Competition is so tremendous that microseconds count; look at Ezor's celebration over a 0.04-second gain in speed. To that end, human performance labs routinely fine-tune players' skills. High-tech instruments calculate the amount of work being done by each muscle group, for example, and recommend changes in gait, body angle, and stance.

Whether teams choose to move a football forward primarily by passing or running seems to cycle with the times, almost like skirt lengths. Today, teams favor passing. Partly this is the result of rule changes that have restricted defensive moves and liberalized offensive moves, presumably to generate more scores.

So, although a rushing game is less popular, use of this strategy can bring unexpected successes because of its surprise element. To that end, coaches keep the team prepared, stressing good muscle development, speed, and running-play offensive line blocking skills.

Muscle Development

Skeletal muscle accounts for about 40 percent of a person's body weight, making it the largest tissue mass in the body. Every movement made is the result of muscle contractions, by a system generally so flawless that it is easily taken for granted.

Our muscles are organized as motor units, each stimulated simultaneously by a single nerve. The number of fibers in a unit can vary tremendously, from as few as ten in the eye muscles, for example, to 100 in the abdomen.

Although it seems as if muscles both stretch and contract, they in fact can only contract, to about 50 percent of their resting length. To stretch, a muscle must either have an outside force exerted on it, or, as happens most often, an opposing muscle contract to provide the "pull" for the stretch. (On a bird, for example, one set of muscles contracts to raise the wind, another set contracts to lower it.) Two types of fibers provide muscle strength: fast-twitch and slow-twitch. Each has characteristics special to it:

• Fast-twitch fibers provide a sharp, strong contraction for a brief (40-millisecond) period. They provide instantaneous, sometimes spectacular, forces. The fibers are well endowed with the enzymes used in anaerobic energy generation. Unfortunately, this type of energy generation is short-lived, so fast-twitch muscles fatigue easily. These muscles prevail in activities requiring a quick burst of strength, such as a 100- or 200-meter sprint. Fullback Larry Csonka, while with the Miami Dolphins, often displayed this type of energy generation with his slow but powerful runs.

• Slow-twitch muscles respond more slowly but contract for a longer period of time (100–200 milliseconds). They favor the aerobic process for energy production, and so are rich in mitochondria. Oxygenated blood makes them redder than fast-twitch fibers. These muscles are most favored for endurance activities such as long-distance running or bicycling on the Tour de France.

An athlete must choose which type of muscle he wants to improve, and train accordingly. Exercise using repetitive motion tends to develop slow-twitch muscles (Greg LeMond), whereas high-intensity, low-repetition work develops the fast-twitch group (Larry Csonka). Individual exercises directed at both types of muscles result in little benefit to either. In other words, any exercise may not be better than none, if an athlete is exercising the wrong type of muscles for the particular sport.

Whether a person has a preponderance of fast-twitch or slow-twitch fibers has long been believed to be genetically determined. Exercise supposedly could increase the size of the fibers (hypertrophy) but could not add new ones (hyperplasia). Some scientists now think differently, William J. Gonyea among them. A physiologist at the University of Texas Health Science Center in Dallas, Gonyea has induced hyperplasia in cats conditioned to lift increasingly heavy weights to receive food. Over a 34-week training period, the cats lifting more than one kilogram (high-resistance group) experienced as much as an 11-percent increase in the diameter of both slow- and fast-twitch fibers, and an overall increase of 20.5 percent in the number of muscle fibers. The low-resistance group (those lifting less than one kilogram) showed no hyperplasia, but did experience hypertrophy in slow-twitch muscles. Gonyea believes the increase may be the result of fiber splitting. In comparison with the control group, neither the high- nor low-resistance group had a significant shift in fiber types or fiber proportions. Although other researchers have backed up Gonyea's findings, questions still exist and more research is needed before the genetic theory is thrown out entirely.

Sprinting

To increase his speed away from the scrimmage line, should running back Emmitt Smith stride faster or stride longer? On a mechanical basis, his running speed is the product of his stride rate and stride length. Analyses show that sprinters achieving their best times usually do so with improved stride rates, rather than lengths, although they were not consciously attempting to change either aspect of their sprint.

The first step off the line takes the most strength, because a runner must produce a large acceleration force to overcome the inertia of his body. After that, speed is developed only when a foot is on the ground, providing a force pushing the body forward. Yet, as a runner gets moving, as much as 60 percent of each stride cycle is spent "in the air," and speed decreases during these intervals. Hence, the more time the feet are on the ground (i.e., more strides versus longer ones), the more speed should be generated.

The fastest runners have not only fast muscles but also a well-coordinated central nervous system. Research shows that the leg extensor muscles are active before the foot meets the ground; therefore, a good sense of timing is crucial. The nervous system must orchestrate the timing of the motor units so that the leg motion matches the speed of the foot along the ground. This skill may be inherited rather than learned, because research has shown that the fastest sprinters move their legs and feet faster than average in other activities besides running—tap dancing, for example.

Offense

Certainly a component essential to a good rushing game is the team's offensive skill. If the quarterback or passer gets trounced too soon, the ball doesn't travel very far. However, muscle mass alone doesn't provide a good block; speed, weight, and balance are equally important. Because a high average carrying distance is only about five yards (Jim Brown holds the record at 5.2), most tackles are clearly successful. Unfortunately, players suffer substantial injuries in exchange for this success rate.

A Stanford University study showed that a collision between two professional football players moving at top speed generates enough energy to move a 33-ton object one inch. (Perhaps more graphically, Gerald Riggs of the Washington Redskins reportedly collided with a Nissan pickup during running practice: the truck suffered $1,370 in damage.) Momentum determines which person ends up sitting on the turf, and whether or not one of the players gets injured depends on the type of surface being played on, how good the player's equipment is, and last, but not least, luck.

Results from biomechanical studies have induced substantial changes both in game rules and in equipment used by the players, sometimes in reverse order from what one might expect. Invention of the plastic helmet in 1939, for example, reduced external head injuries. Unfortunately, it also encouraged players to use their heads in blocking, known as butt blocking. Sports physicians noticed a dramatic increase in the number of head and neck injuries resulting from this technique, some ending in death, and the practice was banned in 1976.

Helmets undoubtedly prevent head injuries, both external and internal, but the latter still pose a grave risk for football players. Stephen E. Reid, a sports physician at Northwestern University Medical School, researched the magnitude of head blows a player could suffer during a game. By wiring accelerometers into a helmet, Reid tested a middle line-backer throughout seven Big Ten conference games. The player suffered 169 head jolts, with forces ranging from 40 to 230 Gs for time periods ranging from 20 to 420 milliseconds. Fifteen of these were rated as high-intensity blows, of a sort likely to cause a concussion or brain damage. One definite concussion occurred. This must have been what Vince Lombardi meant when he said, "Football isn't a contact sport, it's a collision sport. Dancing is a contact sport." (This has also been attributed to Duffy Daugherty.)

Helmets unquestionably reduced the force of these jolts, and modern versions even include a liner made from air bags, inflated with a bicycle pump after the helmet is on the player's head.

Are players who wear black uniforms meaner? Psychologist Thomas Gilovich, of Cornell University, with doctoral student Mark G. Frank, looked at seventeen years of NFL records, 1970 to 1986, to see if there was a pattern. They found that the five teams wearing black at that time (L.A. Raiders, New Orleans Saints, Pittsburgh Steelers, Cincinnati Bengals, and Chicago Bears—who wore navy blue, often perceived as black), incurred more penalty yards than the league-wide average in all but one of the seventeen seasons. Carrying the study one step further, they looked to see if the same situation happened when the teams wore other uniforms (i.e., their reverse colors, or "at home" suits). The effect on the players (or referees) continued: either the players were just as mean, or the referees perceived them to be; either way, they were penalized more than average. Other studies done by Gilovich indicate that spectators as well as referees also have that perception.

So teams playing against black-suited opponents may be particularly interested in the "flak jacket," another recent improvement in equipment. This layered jacket has cylinder-shaped pockets that will, when subjected to sudden changes in air pressure, seal off and form pockets of air that help absorb the impact of a hit. Tests have shown that the jacket, although weighing only 6.5 ounces, can deflect as much as 587 pounds of force per square inch.

Speaking of weight, the assorted equipment a modern football player wears now adds about 12 to 15 pounds to the scales. Fifteen years ago it was significantly more (25 pounds) and has lessened as a result of improved materials.

And the next time you think your spouse is taking too long in getting ready for a party, consider this: it takes a player about two hours to dress for a game.

Artificial Turf

How does a typical football player feel about artificial turf?

"I detest it."

"The guy who invented it should have to sleep on it."

"It definitely shortens careers."

Getting quotes from players about how they feel about artificial turf is easy, and the foregoing are typical. Not as easy, however, is getting quotes from persons who like the stuff. Certainly their statements are not as unequivocal as those of the players.

Probably one of the most controversial issues ever to hit football, the battle over the pros and cons of artificial turf continues to rage, even though almost forty years have passed since the first carpet decorated the Astrodome. Although modified and upgraded through the years, artificial turf is still not universally acclaimed.

The question that can't seem to be answered consistently is: Does artificial turf cause more injuries? Studies abound, but contradict one another.

John W. Powell, Ph.D., research associate at the Department of Orthopedic Surgery at the University of Iowa School of Medicine, analyzed NFL injury data from 1980 to 1985. His conclusion: the odds are greater for injuries to occur on artificial turf than other surfaces. A later report done by James A. Nicholas, MD, and his colleagues, as reported in the *Journal of the American Medical Association*, supported the opposite view: there isn't any difference. His team collected data on seventeen years of play by the New York Jets. A study done by the NCAA, covering National Collegiate Athletic Association games played during 1987, showed that during that year more injuries occurred on natural grass than on artificial turf.

How can what appears to be such a simple question have two opposite answers? Part of the problem is that so many variables exist, making direct comparisons difficult. The turf itself can vary widely with brand, age, and hardness of surface. Older turf deteriorates from ultraviolet radiation, smog, and traffic. Consequently, it losses its "springiness," becoming less shock absorbent and is slicker to play on.

These same variables make it difficult for a player to know how to play on various fields. A related study showed, for example, that the time it takes a shot put to come to rest decreases by 33 percent on five-year-old turf—probably not a serious problem in football, but having a great effect in baseball. What concerns football players more than playing technique is how to avoid injuries. Older turf makes a surface they already consider hard even more difficult to endure. Coach John McKay says, "We think of it as fuzzy concrete." It is significant that many teams still practice on the real stuff.

Excessive traction is most often accused of contributing to the high injury rate. "Typical turf injury occurs when you plant your foot and pivot," says Randy Dick, assistant director of sports sciences for the NCAA. "Your foot stays locked to the surface, but your body continues to rotate, which can cause a knee or ankle injury." On the other hand, "Give me Astroturf any time," says ex-offensive lineman Dan Dierdorf. "When I dig in on Astroturf, I get positive traction. I can concentrate on the play, not my footing."

Turf toe (technically called a metatarsophalangeal joint injury) is a long-lasting injury that has seen a dramatic increase since the advent of artificial turf. One study attributes 83 percent of this type of injury to rugs. The big toe gets pushed up and back so far that ligaments in the joint are torn; in severe cases the toe can actually dislocate. The condition can degenerate into bone spurs and an arthritic condition known as hassux rigidus—a definite career buster. Turf toe usually happens during a tackle, when the foot pivots and another player falls on top of it, causing hyperextension of the joint. On regular grass, the foot slides with relative ease if the player twists his foot; not so on artificial turf, where friction keeps the toe glued to the ground.

The type of shoe worn by a football player can either encourage or help prevent this malady. Flexible rubber-soled shoes are commonly implicated in the injury, whereas special rigid-soled, seven-cleat football shoes help prevent it. Also available are spring-steel inserts that provide important rigidity, helping prevent the foot from overflexing.

Cost is often used to justify the use of artificial turf. It is much more expensive to install initially—$39 per square yard, as compared with $8 for conventional sod—but is claimed to lower maintenance costs by at least 80 percent. These estimates apparently do not consider replacement costs. Boston College tried three brands of turf in fourteen years. The University of Florida also went through three rugs in fourteen years; humidity kept rotting the pad. Some teams have given up on it entirely; the Chicago Bears, for example. Under these circumstances it is debatable whether the installations are actually cost-effective.

Despite the often-heard negative reactions to inorganic greenery, some players love it. Fast runners tend to be even faster, and kickers consistently get off more accurate shots. True, other reasons also apply, but the percentage of successful field goals increased by 40 percent in the last thirty years.

Clearly, even if affection for artificial turf isn't growing, the number of fields sporting it certainly is. Someday, though, we might see more of what George Toma did to Arrowhead Stadium in Kansas city: he planted his Astroturf with grass seed in the hope that the field could qualify for the World Cup game in soccer, which can't be played on artificial turf. In only five days the grass seed, which had been combined with dirt, sprouted and grew a full two inches. Good drainage apparently helped. So artificial turf is good for something after all!

Chapter 9
The Frisbee

An Identified Flying Object

"I held nothing back. I wanted to win, but I wanted even more to be taken to my limit, knowing (if only until the end of the game) that paradise isn't a place where you are the passive recipient of eternal bliss but rather a state of being in which you are offered the incomparable privilege of abandoning caution, of giving your all, of realizing every last shred of your potential."

—George Leonard, *Describing his emotional attachment to Frisbee in* Walking on the Edge of the World

In 1965, two MIT students directed an important question to the Wham-O Company: what special engineering makes a Frisbee fly? The students figured that this company should know, in that it owned the trademark and was the primary manufacturer of the product. The answer, however, took them aback, "Your guess is as good as ours"— or words to that effect. Leonard Silver, one of the students, adds, "They said if we found out why the thing flies that we should let them know."

Wham-O began making the Frisbee in 1957, an auspicious year in that it coincided with the first Sputnik flight and beginning of the Space Age. The first Frisbees out of the mold were called Pluto Platters, reputedly a name coined by inventor Fred Morrison because the discs carried the names of the planets. However, Rich Knerr, one of the cofounders of Wham-O, refutes this story, stating that he named the disc after a cartoon character.

Another story has long circulated that Wham-O named the disc after the now-defunct Frisbie Pie Company, of Bridgeport, Connecticut. Students from nearby Yale University reportedly played with discarded pie tins, shouting "Frisbie!"

By whatever name, the science of flying discs has so tantalized aficionados of the sport that during the eighties universities offered special courses on the subject. Instructor D. William ("Willie") Williams is given credit for the first such class, titled Disc Skills 105, and officially accredited at Arizona State University in 1981.

William's program first had to pass muster with the University's physical education department. Approval from the physics department probably would have been more appropriate, because where else can a student learn about aerodynamics, airfoils, angular momentum, forward and rotational velocity, Newton's law, gyroscopic stability and precession, and the effects of weather on flying? Quite a program, but Williams believes that an understanding of the subjects enables students to play better.

It may seem that a Frisbee's flight should be easy to analyze. After all, it's merely a spinning piece of plastic. But in reality, the forces are complex.

The disc's propensity for "turning over" particularly frustrates both throwers and disc designers. Similar in this respect to a boomerang, turnover is due to processional forces acting on the Frisbee's spin plane. (Precession is discussed in detail in Chapter 5.) A flying disc encounters changes in rotational velocity (which leads to precession) because even distribution of lift occurs on it. Two principles come into play: Bernoulli's equations, which relate differences in air speed to differences in air pressure, and the Magnus effect, a principle which states that the existence of different air pressures will produce a force acting from the region of high pressure to the region of low pressure **(see Figure 9–1)**.

On a flying disc, this force develops because (1) as the air hits the front of the disc it is effectively split into two layers, one above and one below, and (2) the slightly domed shape of the Frisbee forces the air on top of the disc to travel farther and therefore faster than the air on the bottom part of the disc. Lower air pressure results at the top and hence lift is created.

But, what goes up, must come down. Whenever an object flies through the air, gravity and drag exert an irresistible attraction that cannot be denied. Drag is a force generated parallel to and in an opposite direction of an object's motion. It is generally proportionate to the

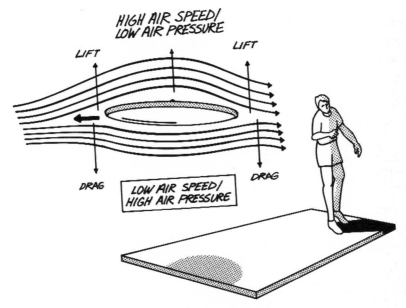

9-1 *Principles that Power a Frisbee (Air Speed and Pressure). Bernoulli's theorem tells us that air traveling at fast speeds, such as the air above a flying Frisbee, has less pressure than air traveling at slower speeds, such as air below a Frisbee, and lift is consequently generated. The Magnus effect, the force that acts from a region of high pressure to a region of low pressure, explains the Frisbee's tendency to deflect in the direction of its spin.*

amount of lift generated, so a disc with more lift will also suffer more drag, causing it to slow down faster. The best designed discs compromise these two forces.

Precessional forces and the tendency of a disc to turn over pose a larger problem, however, not only for players attempting a perfect throw, but for the scientists and designers attempting to eliminate this tendency. Mace Schuurmans, a former Swiss Frisbee-throwing champion, while in medical school wrote a report on the aerodynamics of a flying disc. At the time he thought a solution to the turnover problem was obvious: "Just make the center of gravity and the center of lift of a disc coincide and there would be no gyroscopic precession." Later, in laboratory experiments, he realized that such a solution was impossible to achieve with current knowledge and technology. "The patterns of flow around a spinning disc were far more complex than I had ever imagined."

9-2   *Hover Flight. For a "hover flight" or a "floater," the thrower faces into the wind and uses a backhand throw or release.*

So, for now, Frisbee throwers will have to live with the turnover effect. A talented thrower can compensate for precessional forces, to a certain extent, by initially launching the disc with a tilt in a direction opposite to the precession angle. Called "adjusting the hyzer angle," a disc with clockwise spin is released with its left side tilted down, a disc with counterclockwise spin with its right side down.

For a "hover flight" or a "floater," the thrower faces into the wind and uses a backhand throw **(see Figure 9–2)**. If the disk is thrown forward and slightly up, it will make a high climb and a slow fall. To make a disc dip and move sideways in the air, the thrower uses a thumb grip (thumb on the bottom of the disk and fingers on top). The wrist is bent until the disc is touching the arm and the elbow is cocked back. During the throw, the arm is brought forward and the wrist uncocked at the point of release, imparting a sharp snap to the Frisbee. This throw (called the thumber or thumb flip) is particularly hard to catch **(see Figure 9-3)**.

Other throwing techniques can affect the characteristics of a flight. High rates of spin help a freestyle thrower maintain control of the disc; orientation and forward speed are more important to a distance thrower. (An average thrower gives a spinning disc an initial rotational velocity of about 8 revolutions per second; professionals can, depending on ambient flying conditions, generate up to 16 revolutions per second.)

Freestyle artists appreciate a recent invention called the SpinJAMMER. Californian Michael Sandeen's flying disc incorporates a sunken cone in its center that allows ultra-easy spinning (called "stalling" by disc enthusiasts), and acrobatic maneuvers that formerly took years to perfect can now be mastered in days. Sandeen benefited from Wham-O's patent expiration. His impressive success with the SpinJAMMER probably sent executives of Wham-O into a tailspin, but they were as helpless to do anything about it as a Frisbee is in avoiding forces of precession and drag.

Yet Wham-O endures, as do Sunday afternoon games at the park. And although Frisbee played among friends or with a friendly pup may not require much stamina, such isn't the case for players of Ultimate Frisbee.

Played on a field 120 yards long and 40 yards wide, the players pass the disc to one another, advancing down the field until they gain a point. Points result when one of the two seven-person team members completes a pass into the opponent's end zone, 25 yards from the end of the field. Dropping the disc or throwing it out of bounds moves control of it to the other team.

Ultimate players can easily encounter three- and four-minute intense sprints for each point, because the disc is typically passed short distances at each throw, rather than by long, field-length throws. If the disc ends up changing teams before a point is made, another three-minute sprint can easily ensue. Superior lung capacity and strong legs are a must! Not only that, but as Jon Bowermaster wrote for *Sports Illustrated*, "When club teams play Ultimate, the resulting melee requires that a player have the quickness of a basketball point guard, the

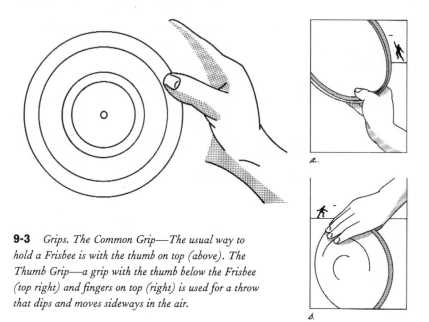

9-3   *Grips. The Common Grip—The usual way to*
hold a Frisbee is with the thumb on top (above). The
Thumb Grip—a grip with the thumb below the Frisbee
(top right) and fingers on top (right) is used for a throw
that dips and moves sideways in the air.

finesse of a hockey player, the blocking techniques of a football guard, and the reactions of a soccer goalie. A willingness to hit the dirt—teeth first, without pads—is essential."

Internationally, the World Flying Disc Federation, headquartered in Sweden, actively promotes flying disc competitions. Its annual tournaments feature both individual and team events. Run and catch contests dare an individual to throw a disc as far as possible and then catch it one-handed; freestyle events feature acrobatics and dancing as graceful as any ballet. Maximum distance and maximum time aloft competitions are also held.

Whether playing on a competitive level or just for fun, a player frustrated with turnover or high winds may choose to turn the disc into a food platter. That's what orphans in Angola did when Wham-O sent Sister Dominique, a nun working there, 7,000 discs. The Sister responded with this message: "The dishes you sent were wonderful. We eat all our meals off them. And the most amazing thing happened. Some of the children are throwing them as sort of a game. This may be an idea for you."

What a lovely idea.

Chapter 10
Gliding

The Gentle Science Behind Motion and Air Currents

"Soaring—call it an art or a sport—the ability to stay aloft in near-silent, powerless flight for hour upon hour and mile upon mile, man alone among the birds, is an experience without equal in our modern technology-oriented world."

—*Paul Garrison*
From Gliders

What's it like to soar on the wings of the wind? Forget motors and fumes—glider pilots use air currents as fuel. No small forces, these: they can rapidly swoosh a plane up to 30,000 feet (the record is 49,009).

Although the FAA considers gliders and sailplanes to be one and the same, some sailplane owners will adamantly argue otherwise. To them, gliders are meant only to descend slowly from their launch points. Sailplanes, on the other hand, actually soar, gaining altitude after their release by hitching a ride on rising air currents. As the risk of insulting some sailplane owners, the terms are used interchangeably here.

Gliders stay in the air for the same reason that airplanes do: lift develops from the movement of air across the wings **(see Figure 10-1)**. Adequate air movement, combined with an appropriate angle of attack, generates a sufficient excess of lift over drag to permit flight. If the plane slows down too much or its positive angle of attack is too large (nose too high above the center of gravity), the plane will quit flying and stall. Both airplanes and gliders are designed for stability, however, so if a stall occurs the nose will come down, whether or not the pilot intervenes, and the plane will gather speed until control resumes. However, the pilot's action can prevent the plane from going into a spin.

Gliders have proportionately longer wingspans than airplanes, both to maximize lift and minimize drag, and to provide a longer glide ratio.

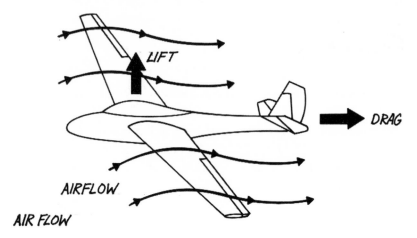

10-1 *Forces Acting on a Glider. Gliders stay in the air for the same reason that airplanes do — lift develops from the movement of air across their wings.*

Training planes typically have wingspans of about 40 feet and a glide ratio of about 23 to 1, meaning that, without rising air currents, for every 23 feet the plane moves forward, it will drop in altitude 1 foot. Theoretically then, such a plane at 2,500 feet can travel about 11 miles before having to land. High-performance planes boast wingspans of up to 80 feet, allowing glide ratios of nearly 60 to 1.

A glider pilot stays on the alert for three types of lift to fuel his climb toward the sky: thermal lifts, ridge (slope) lift, and mountain waves. Thermals are rising columns of air that develop from an uneven heating of the earth's surface, such as occur above paved parking lots or unusually dry fields **(see Figure 10-2)**. Ridge lift occurs when a strong wind blows over a ridge, causing an updraft. This wind must be blowing at least 10 mph **(see Figure 10-3)**.

The strongest lift of all comes from mountain waves, formed when winds hit a mountain and generate a standing-air wave, so named because the wave stops in one place while the stable air forming it passes through. (Similar in effect to the way an eddy is formed in a creek when water flows around a rock.) As shown in **Figure 10-4**, the descending air rebounds and forms a primary wave, which is stationary with respect to the ground. Sailplanes literally "surf" along the face of

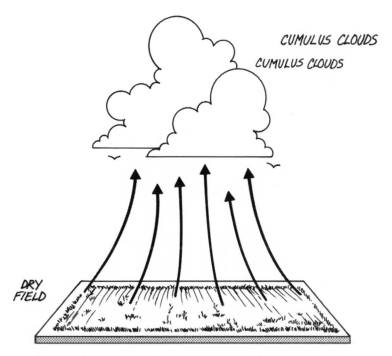

10-2 *Thermal Lift. A thermal lift is a rising column of air that develops from an uneven heating of the earth's surfaces above such areas as paved parking lots or unusually dry fields.*

this wave as they climb upward. Underneath and between the primary and secondary waves, turbulent air flows in a horizontal vortex, called a rotor.

All current altitude records recorded by sailplanes can be credited to wave soarers. Only experienced pilots take advantage of such waves because lift rates of up to 2,000 feet per minute can rapidly propel a plane past the 14,000-foot level, where auxiliary oxygen becomes necessary.

One of the most famous mountain waves is the Bishop Wave that forms over Owens Valley, California. High-velocity winds, formed in the wake of a fast-moving cold front, blow down from the Sierra Nevada mountains, hit the desert floor, and then rush upward in tremendously strong updrafts. These waves enable a pilot to climb to heights

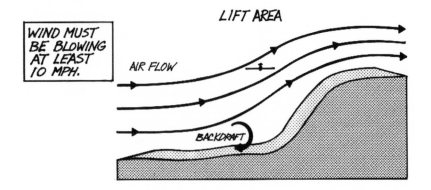

LIFT AREA LIFT

10-3 *Ridge Lift. Ridge lift occurs when a strong wind (at least 10 mph) blows over a ridge, causing an updraft.*

of 40,000 feet or higher. The weather system affecting Bishop first passes through Seattle, Washington, so pilots can predict good wave conditions a day or so in advance.

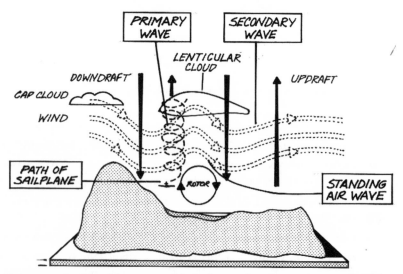

10-4 *Mountain Wave. The strongest lift of all comes from "mountain waves," which generate a standing airwave, stationary with respect to the ground, along which sailplanes soar as they climb upward.*

To spot thermals, a pilot looks for dust devils (but not those made from moving vehicles) and growing cumulus clouds. High-soaring birds, such as hawks and buzzards, indicate the presence of rising air. Physical evidence on the ground, such as smoke or flags, can also supply clues, although a pilot must spot two separate sources for the signal to be useful. If the two indicators (perhaps smoke) are blowing toward one another, an uprising current should exist between them; if they are blowing away from each other, downdrafts are likely.

Cumulus clouds mark the top of individual thermals. Experience teaches pilots to discern which clouds are still growing, and thus have rising air. A lucky pilot will encounter a row of these clouds, enabling him to jump from thermal to thermal. The stronger mountain waves produce lenticular clouds, smooth, flat circular clouds that resemble flying saucers.

Since most thermals have small diameters, a pilot attempts to stay within the rising air as long as possible by executing tight turns at bank angles of 30 to 40 degrees. Downdrafts occur between the thermals; hence, the pilot speeds the plane up (by angling the plane's nose down) to lessen the time spent in these areas.

Pilots accustomed to the high noise level encountered in regular airplanes may find a glider so quiet that they begin to mentally rehearse engine-failure procedures. For those expecting total quiet, though, a surprise is in store. Two types of noises often startle a first-time flier: the rush of wind against the plane, which varies with the airspeed, and the sounds the plane makes as it flexes under various flight loads. Air leaks cause noises as air flows out of the cabin on a fast climb and leaks in on a fast descent. Wings "load up" when the plane encounters a strong thermal or when the pilot maneuvers a tight turn, and then "unload" as these stresses reduce. The resulting "snap-crackle-pop" sounds, especially those made by metal-skinned wings, may scare the uninitiated.

Sailplanes are structurally very strong, and usually built to withstand stresses about twelve times their own weight. Fiberglass is the material of choice, with Kevlar used for highly stressed parts. To facilitate transportation on the ground, the wings and tail section are usually removable.

Until recently, gliders were made as light as possible, and today's designs that make lightness the main criterion are called floaters. As faster speeds became more important than long-distance range, wing loading became more important than overall weight. Wing load is the total weight of the plane divided by its wing area. A floater typically has a wing loading of about 2.5 pounds per square foot, but modern "lead sleds" go as high as 12 pounds per square foot. Each is quite different in terms of speed: a floater may go only 100 mph, but a plane using modern design and materials may go 170 mph. (For a glider, the only compensating force against drag is a component of gravity along the glide slope, and this force can only be increased by making the plane heavier.) The ultra-smooth surfaces provided by modern composite materials also contribute to higher speeds. It takes stronger thermals to lift these heavier planes, however, so not all of them are appropriate for long distance, cross-country flights.

On sailplanes, distribution of passenger weight is critical. Most gliders accommodate pilots up to six feet tall and weighing up to 220 pounds, although those with long legs or backs may find the seats uncomfortable. A pilot weighing under 145 pounds will probably require additional ballast, because a plane must have a minimum weight (as shown on its placard) to fly safely. Extra weight moves the center of gravity forward, making the plane easier to fly.

Conversely, stalling and spinning characteristics will be worse, and possibly even dangerous if there is not enough weight or the weight on the plane is too far back.

Sailplanes fly considerably slower than regular airplanes. Even so, a pilot must maintain a minimum speed of about 40 knots, or 45 mph, to generate sufficient lift to keep flying. (One knot equals one nautical mile per hour, or roughly 100 feet per minute.) Most training gliders have a normal flying speed of about 50 mph. A normal rate of descent at this speed is 150 to 200 feet per minute. The faster the glider is moving, the greater the rate of descent (sinking rate), because the plane will be gliding at a steeper angle. Of course, a pilot tries to find updrafts to compensate for this lost altitude.

Compared to most airplanes, the cockpit of a sailplane looks spartan, with few controls and instruments to master before a pilot takes to the

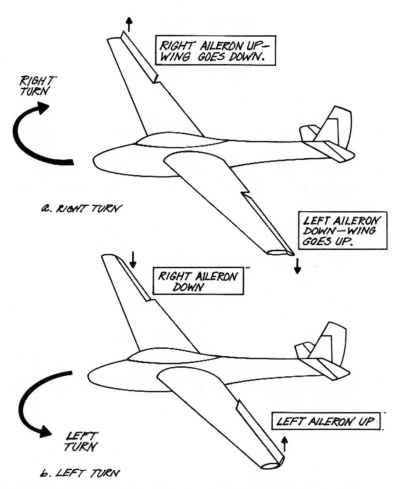

10-5 *Turning a Plane. The pilot moves the control stick in the direction he wants to turn. For a right turn, the right aileron goes up and the left aileron down. For a left turn, it's the reverse.*

skies. One similarity between them, though, is a three-axis control. A control stick (or control column) both turns (banks) the plane left or right and raises or lowers the nose. Moving the stick forward or backward changes the pitch of the plane by moving the elevator, which is located on the tail. Depressing the elevator (stick back) forces the nose of the plane up, and raising the elevator (stick forward), pushes the nose down.

To bank or turn the plane, the pilot moves the control stick in the direction he wants to turn. This action moves the ailerons, small flaps located on the wing tips. Pushing the stick to the left causes the aileron on the left wing to lose lift and the one on the right to gain lift, effectively raising the right wing and lowering the left, hence forcing a left turn. Thus, to control either pitch or direction, the pilot moves the stick in the direction he wants to go **(see Figure 10–5)**.

A dropped aileron creates added resistance to the airflow, which makes the nose of the plane tend to point a few degrees away from the direction of the turn, a tendency called yawing. The rudder, located on the tail and controlled by foot pedals, helps push the tail of the plane around, thus coordinating the turn. Because of their long wing spans, gliders produce much more yaw than regular airplanes, and more rudder action is necessary, especially in the beginning of turns.

The instrument panel on a sailplane includes a compass, an airspeed indicator, altimeter, and variometer (VSI—vertical speed indicator), which measures the rate of climb or descent. Many glider pilots consider the variometer the most important instrument because it enables them to detect rising air and to find the best position for experiencing maximum lift. Using this instrument, a pilot "maps" out the thermal, by noticing where climbing is experienced and where it fades out, and ultimately ascertaining where the center of lift exists. This "centering" may take a novice a few minutes to accomplish, but experts can often do it in a minute or less. Constant adjustment is then required to stay in the center of the thermal.

In the United States, gliders are usually launched by aerotow. A 150- to 200-foot cable connects the glider to an airplane, which pulls it up to about 3,000 feet. The pilot of the glider then pulls a release knob that disconnects the cable. In Europe, winch launches are commonplace. There, a glider is pulled forward and aloft by a 1,500-foot cable attached to a 200-hp winch. In either case, gaining an altitude of at least 200 feet is critical because, should the cable break, a pilot needs this much room to maneuver a turn and return to the landing strip.

To get around the difficulties of launching, motor gliders are now popular, especially for training flights. Some of these planes are gliders with an add-on motor; others are high-performance aircraft that handle like a glider. After climbing under power, the propeller blades are feathered (turned on edge) to reduce drag. The biggest benefit of using motor gliders for training is that many "touch and goes" (the pilot lands momentarily on the field and immediately takes off again) can be made in a single day. A pilot can rapidly gain takeoff and landing experience this way; still, most students look forward to advancing to nonmotorized flights.

Glider pilots must be expert at landing; without a motor, they have only one chance at it. Care must also be taken to avoid drifting too far downwind of the airport, or the landing is likely to take place in a farmer's field. To land, a pilot usually brings the plane in higher than needed and then uses dive brakes (also called airbrakes or speedbrakes) to increase the drag but not speed when the pilot goes into a steep final descent. These brakes are vertical "fences" that raise and lower out of the wings. Older planes used flaps on the wings, called spoilers, for this purpose, but these are not as effective as speedbrakes.

Chapter 11
Golf

The Game That Traps the Masses

"Cursed be the hand that made these holes!"

—*William Shakespeare*
Richard III

Environmentalists may think they have a serious problem—running out of landfill areas—but the acreage they need is a fraction of what golfers need; they're running out of fairways. Teeing off has become such a popular pastime in the United States that even if one new golf course were build every day until the year 2010, it wouldn't satisfy the demand. Every year, 2.5 million neophytes join the more than 25 million who already play. (Maybe the solution is to advertise the difficulty of the game, and stress the effect of frustration on blood pressure.)

Two questions that inevitably enter these neophytes' mind are: Why is a golf ball dimpled, and why does a golfer carry around so many clubs? They soon learn that both are attempts to control that pesky ball's flight, and to move the ball from tee to hole in as few strokes as possible.

How far and in what direction a ball travels primarily depends on the club selected, and on the force and spin imparted to the ball on impact. How well a player manages these three variables makes the difference between a birdie, par, or bogie. Secondary influences include the type of ball used and, to a lesser degree, on whether the club's grooves are U- or V-shaped.

Dimples on a golf ball increase its flight time, and hence its distance, by affecting the pattern of air flow surrounding the ball as it sails through the air. The layer of air closest to the ball is the boundary layer. If this layer experiences laminar flow (which typically happens on a smooth ball), the air layer tends to separate and break away from the ball easily. Because this separation can happen early—sometimes before the air gets even half the distance to the back of the ball—it causes a large wake of low pressure to form behind the ball, resulting in a high drag force. On the other hand, if the air layer is turbulent (as it will be with a rough ball), the turbulent boundary layer mixes rapidly with the air next to it. The boundary layer under this condition doesn't get a chance to slow down (it is getting constant momentum from the outside layer of air), and thus tends to hug the ball, resulting in a smaller wake of low pressure and so less drag **(see Figures 11–1a & b).**

The dimples on an airborne golf ball, therefore, reduce drag forces considerably—by about half—and the ball travels up to 75 percent farther than if it were smooth. Unfortunately, the dimples also amplify the forces that cause hooks and slices.

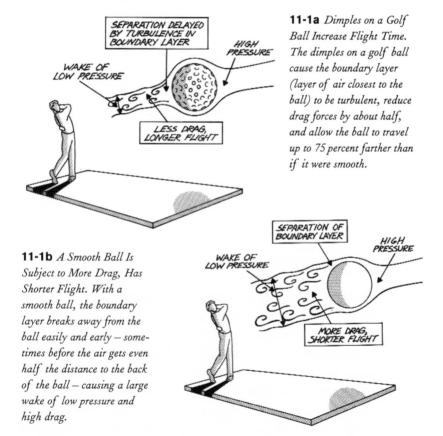

11-1a *Dimples on a Golf Ball Increase Flight Time. The dimples on a golf ball cause the boundary layer (layer of air closest to the ball) to be turbulent, reduce drag forces by about half, and allow the ball to travel up to 75 percent farther than if it were smooth.*

11-1b *A Smooth Ball Is Subject to More Drag, Has Shorter Flight. With a smooth ball, the boundary layer breaks away from the ball easily and early – sometimes before the air gets even half the distance to the back of the ball – causing a large wake of low pressure and high drag.*

Although all golf balls have approximately 400 dimples, a player still must choose among four types of construction: (1) two-piece solid ball, (2) liquid-center wound ball, (3) solid-core wound ball, and (4) multilayer ball.

A two-piece solid ball is designed to leave the clubface with less backspin and a higher initial velocity. This translates into more distance. Less backspin also means less sidespin, so the so-called "distance" balls reduce the curvature of a slice or hook. It consists of a hard cover over a large core, whose resiliencies vary by ball.

The liquid-center wound ball has soft cover over rubber windings wrapped around a liquid core. It is for golfers who seek feel and workability in lieu of distance. It has a high spin rate, which brings good news and bad news: it produces control and workability but magnifies a slice or hook.

The solid-core wound ball consists of a soft cover over a thin layer of rubber windings and a large rubber core. This ball flies nearly the distance of the two-piece ball and the rubber windings increase the spin rate off short irons. Golfers who play with this ball give up a little distance in exchange for control.

The multilayer ball is a three-piece ball that features a large, solid core, a thin, firm inner layer and a soft but durable cover. On iron shots, the inner layer is designed to work with the cover to produce a high spin rate. Off the driver the core comes more into play, with the inner layer having less effect. On tee shots the multilayer ball performs much like a two-piece ball, resulting in less spin and more distance.

The club chosen for a shot greatly affects the ball's ensuing flight pattern. The rules allow pro golfers to carry up to fourteen clubs, which are chosen from the wood (numbered one to five), from the irons (numbered one to nine), and from special-purpose clubs (wedges and putters). Woods are selected to achieve long distances down the fairway and irons for shorter, more accurate shots. Wedges are used close to the green (usually 120 yard or less and often to propel balls from sand traps) and off rough ground; putters are used on the green, and occasionally from slightly off the green.

Golf clubs have either wooden heads (woods) or steel heads (irons), although some modern "woods" are made of composite material, steel, or a combination thereof. Many players looked down their noses at them, until

1984 when Lee Trevino won the PGA championship using a metal driver. Curtis Strange has sworn that a metal wood adds 15 yards to his drive.

This extra drive comes from "fully charged" balls. To a physicist, this means a complete transfer of kinetic energy from the club to the ball. Wood, claims John Zebelean, who designed the first steel wood, produces a poor transfer of kinetic energy. But steel, he says, "transfers a tremendous impulse of energy to the ball and charges it at a faster rate. So you have less loss of energy." He also believes that metal woods increase a player's accuracy, because they shorten the time the ball is in contact with the club face, thereby lessening the ball's susceptibility to bad hits caused by the shaft flexing or the ball being hit off center.

The face of each club is inclined at a different angle so that each gives a different loft to the ball. Loft is the angle between a line perpendicular to the face of the clubhead and the horizontal. The degree of loft determines in large part the ensuing trajectory of the ball **(see Figure 11–2)**.

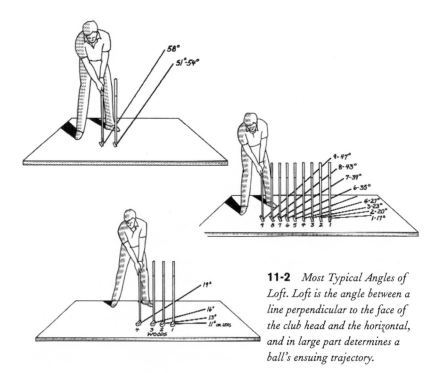

11-2 *Most Typical Angles of Loft. Loft is the angle between a line perpendicular to the face of the club head and the horizontal, and in large part determines a ball's ensuing trajectory.*

Table 11-1 shows typical loft angles for each club and the average range of distance gained by a ball hit by each. Although these angles are the industry standard, variance of up to 8 degrees exist among manufacturers.

Table 11 - 1 Loft Angle and Range per Club			
	MOST TYPICAL ANGLE OF LIFT (DEGREES)	AVERAGE RANGE OF DISTANCE (YARDS) TRAVELED BY THE BALL BY MEN	BY WOMEN
Woods			
No. 1 (driver)	11	220-300	160-180
No. 2 (brassie)	13	210-250	155-170
No. 3 (spoon)	16	200-230	150-170
No. 4	19	190-220	145-165
Irons			
No. 1	17	190-220	145-165
No. 2	20	180-210	140-155
No. 3	23	170-190	135-150
No. 4	27	155-175	125-140
No. 5	31	140-155	115-130
No. 6	35	125-145	110-120
No. 7	39	120-140	100-110
No. 8	43	110-125	90-100
No. 9	47	90-120	70-80
Wedges			
Pitching	51-54	70-100	50-85
Sand	58	—	—
Putter	0-4	—	—

These distances are calculated assuming a calm day at the course. The lightest club is the driver; the heaviest is the putter. Although a driver is lighter than the other clubs, it imparts more momentum to the ball than the irons because it is longer and its weight is concentrated in the club head.

Graphite, a club material that debuted in the early seventies but never caught on, has increased in popularity as a premier component in golf club shafts. A manufacturer heats this carbon material to almost 5,000° F, usually combining it with an epoxy resin to form to composite. Boron is sometimes used, which is twice as stiff as steel but only one-third as heavy. Studies have shown that a ball hit by a graphite driver will go approximately three yards farther than one hit by a steel driver.

The velocity imparted to a ball on impact certainly affects how far it will travel. Although a golf ball's maximum initial speed is about 171 mph (the official rules allow no more than 174), 125 mph is closer to what an average golfer achieves. Most pros, however, obtain 150 mph with their drivers and 120 with their irons. It takes a force of 660 pounds to make the ball leave the tee at 150 mph—no small accomplishment.

When a club comes in contact with a golf ball, it transfers two types of energy: linear (for distance) and rotational (for spin). Each hit generates only so much energy, and the more going to rotation, the less available for distance. On the other hand, backspin enables a ball to fly on a flatter trajectory, because it counteracts the ball's tendency to fall, and once the ball hits the ground, it will roll farther.

Players successful at golf have undoubtedly learned to make spin work for them. The first step in acquiring this skill is to understand how spin influences the flight of the ball; then a player can learn how to impart the appropriate spin.

When a ball is hit dead on, pure backspin is imparted. Up to 8,000 rpm can be generated. The angled face of the club pinches against the ball and makes it rotate backward, toward the club. For just a millisecond, the ball actually climbs up the face of the club. The grooves on the clubface help generate backspin because they increase the amount of friction between the ball and the club. Conversely, wet conditions decrease friction and so reduce backspin. A head wind increases backspin; a tail wind decreases it. William Gobush, manager of aerodynamics research at the Acushnet Company, which makes both Titleist (wound) and Pinnacle (two-piece) balls, has shown that balate-wound balls stay on the clubface microseconds longer than two-piece balls and hence have a faster spin rate.

Rotational forces generated by backspin increase the amount of lift

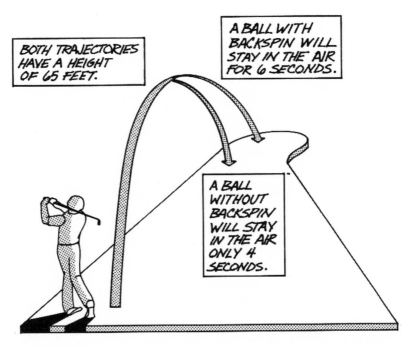

11-3 *Backspin Versus No Backspin. Rotational forces generated by backspin increase the amount of lift experienced by a golf ball. The extra two seconds generated by backspin can equate to as much as 30 yards on the course.*

experienced by a golf ball; therefore, if a ball with backspin has the same trajectory as one without backspin, it will stay in the air longer. For example, if both trajectories have a height of 65 feet, a ball with backspin will stay in the air for six seconds; one without backspin for only four seconds. These two seconds can equate to as much as 30 yards on the course **(see Figure 11–3)**.

A ball's rate of spin is partially dependent on its coefficient of spin, which is determined by the relationship between the ball's core and its cover. A ball having a harder core relative to its cover will spin faster. Traditional Surlyn-covered, two-piece balls spin more slowly than balate-covered balls. Softer covers spin faster. This factor is particularly significant on the green because a two-piece ball will roll farther than a wound ball.

Also contributing to additional spin are U-shaped grooves on the clubface (although this aspect remains somewhat controversial) and the placement of weight on the clubhead. Traditionally, clubs have used V-shaped grooves (before 1984 the rules required them), but since the advent of investment casting (molten steel is poured into ceramic molds) of irons, shallow U-shaped grooves are more popular. Some players claim that U-shaped grooves lessen the effect of wet grass on spin, and so prevent "flyers." (A flyer is a shot that resists the effect of the grooves because grass gets between the ball and the face of the club.)

As previously noted, a ball hit squarely by the face of the club experiences pure backspin, but if a player angles the face of the club at all, sidespin is also generated. A counterclockwise spin will cause the ball to veer left (hook); a clockwise spin will cause it to veer right (slice). If sidespin is deliberately initiated and controlled, to miss an obstacle on the course, for example, the play is called fade (left) or draw (right). If a player does this well—that is, consistently—it's a sure sign that many hours have been spent practicing. (On the other hand, golfer Miller Barber says, "I don't say my golf game is bad, but if I grew tomatoes, they'd come up sliced.")

The flexibility of a club's shaft also affects the distance a ball travels. Just as a rubber band pulled tight stores elastic energy, so a club stores energy as it flexes. When the club and ball collide, this energy is released, giving the ball a higher initial speed and more loft. Wilson Sporting Goods Company recently introduced a line of shafts that they say are tailored to a player's swing. Made of a composition of boron and graphite, the shafts have a high modulus of elasticity; that is, a constant ratio of unit stress to unit deformation. The company offers three types: the stiffest one is for players who have swings faster than 100 mph, the second stiffest for those with swings from 85 to 100 mph, and the third stiffest for wings slower than 85 mph. Other companies rate shaft flex as ladies (L), flexible (A), regular (R), stiff (S), extra stiff (X), and double extra stiff (XX). The stiffer the flex, the more speed and strength a player needs to make the shaft straighten out on impact. More-flexible shafts enable players who have weaker arms and wrists to generate increased club head speed through the club's whipping action.

Sole weighting is another recent "improvement" that is meant to endow a club with more backspin capabilities. By concentrating the club's weight below the center of the ball, more lift is generated on impact. This is another improvement that, unless players are quite consistent in their play, can actually be a detriment. (Sometimes backspin is not desired; for example, when hitting the ball against a prevailing breeze.)

Golfers generally prefer sunny days on the course. Experience has probably shown them that the weather influences the way a ball plays; on a cold day wound balls are harder and fly less far. Players in Alaska take note: two-piece balls are less susceptible to weather changes.

Warm-blooded human beings aren't the only species that enjoy golf courses. At the Jinga Course in Uganda, Africa, a special rule states that "if a ball comes to rest in the dangerous proximity of a crocodile, another ball may be dropped." (One wonders what is the interpretation of "dangerous.") Closer to home, at the Glen Canyon Course in Page, Arizona, the rules states that "if your ball lands with a club's length of a rattlesnake, you're allowed to move the ball." (How about dropping a new one instead, please?) It may be that these critters are drawn to the cooler temperatures found on a golf course, which in a desert can be as much as eight to nine degrees less than the temperature of the surrounding area.

Excuses for lousy scores run riot in the clubhouse. Stephen Leacock, in a satirical essay, "Mathematics for Golfers," calculated the odds that his friend Jones, a habitual excuse-giver, would have a day without difficulties at the golf course. Leacock used these assumptions: (1) Jones was subject to fifty different difficulties, each of which was likely to happen once every ten days, and (2) Jones plays four games of golf a week. Using applications of permutations and probabilities, Leacock calculated how often Jones should not have a good excuse for blowing his game. The answer: once every 2,930,000 years. Leacock adds, "From watching Jones play, I think this is about right."

Putting

Many a golfer meets his nemesis at the green. Percentage-wise, putting makes up a large part of the game. Pros use their putters an average of thirty times a round, so this play makes up about 43 percent of their games.

Some golfers, even pros, become irate when they miss a putt. A recent study by the PGA should console them, however. It found that tour players make only 54.8 percent of the putts attempted from 6 feet; they make only 33.5 percent of those from 10 feet; and at 15 feet, it gets quite abysmal—only 16.8 percent are made. Perhaps even more interesting, the study found that pros tend to do better when the shot is for par, compared to for birdie. Apparently, being at par exerts an effective mental pressure on the player that pays off.

Other research that may help a duffer on the green was done by Brian W. Holmes, of the Department of Physics at San Jose State University, who developed a computer model to determine how a golf ball and hole interact. His findings:

- If a ball is rolling without slipping, it must be moving at 5.34 feet per second (ft/sec) or less to be captured. Otherwise, it has enough velocity to sustain a straight-line path across the top of the hole.
- If the velocity is less than 4.31 ft/sec, the ball will be captured before it reaches the opposite rim of the cup.
- Between 4.31 and 5.34 ft/sec, the ball will hit the opposite rim. Its action then depends on how much the ball bounces and on how much friction is generated from the ball's rotation against the rim.
- If a ball is bouncing or skidding (a propensity for which varies from green to green), it will be captured at greater speeds. This is because a skidding ball has less angular momentum, which can provide "kick" to bounce the ball out of the hole.
- British balls (which are fractionally smaller than U.S. balls: a 1.62-inch diameter compared to a 1.68-inch diameter) are more easily captured.

Holmes' research also found that it is a little easier to sink a wound ball than a two-piece ball.

The above analysis holds for balls directed straight at the hole. Off-center collisions are more complex, and although Holmes has developed equations that show different reactions from different angles of attack, it is beyond the scope of this book to go into them.

Dave Pelz, author of several books and a technical consultant for *Golf Magazine*, has extensively studied putting. Here following are a few pointers from Pelz on the art and science of putting:

> The putter face must be square to the target line at the moment of impact. Otherwise, 90 percent of the deviation is imparted to the ball; that is, for a 20-foot putt, if the face is 10 degrees off, the ball will miss the hole by about three feet. Hit the ball with the "sweet spot" of the club. If you miss this spot by a quarter of an inch, 95 percent of your error will translate to the ball. For any putt longer than eight feet, this error will make you miss the cup.

To find the sweet spot on your club, hold the putter by the top of its grip, between your index finger and thumb, like a plumb line. Take a golf tee and tap the face of the putter, beginning with the toe end, then the heel, and gradually zeroing in on the point at which the putter head swings straight back, twisting neither inward nor outward. This area is the sweet spot. (Although some clubs have a directional line on top of the putter, these marks don't always coincide with the sweet spot, so checking it can be worthwhile.) Years ago this spot was the size of a dime, but today it can be as large as an Oreo cookie.

Also important for accurate putts is a proper length of club. Some pros say that a club is the right length if, when you take your normal stance, only and inch or less of space is between your top hand and the top of the club.

Perhaps as important as technique is a player's mental attitude on the green. The popularity of Timothy Gallwey's *The Inner Game of Golf* shows that there is much more to developing a proper mental attitude than just "thinking positive." Specifically, Gallwey offers exercises meant to increase concentration, confidence, and will power.

Still, merely thinking positive does have an effect. Dave Stockton, the 1970 and 1976 PGA champion, is known for his positive mental attitude. His belief: "I think I deserve to get the ball in the hole every time I stand over a putt." Contrast this attitude with Mac O'Grady, who says putting is driving him from the game. "When I putt, my emotions collide like tectonic plates."

Theories on learning certainly are pertinent to the game of golf. Otherwise, why bother practicing driving or putting? It was formerly believed that the repetitive practice of a motor function would cut a deeper groove in the brain, making recall more spontaneous and accurate. This theory was discarded when it was discovered that memories in the brain are not stored in one central bank, but are dispersed throughout the gray matter. The spinal cord may even store some memories (possibly explaining why a chicken runs around with its head cut off).

However we store the memories, practice definitely encourages a better golf game. Still, it is only a valid exercise if we program the correct movements into the brain. Knowing whether the movement is correct, and storing it in a retrievable manner, entails receiving immediate feedback. Such feedback is difficult if a person is practicing alone at the driving range. Dr. Ralph Mann has tackled this problem and perfected a program that both generates and manipulates feedback in a highly beneficial way.

One question that golfers frequently have is whether they should look at the golf ball or the hole when putting. Studies in 1985 by Gwendolyn Aksamit and in 1980 by I. M. Cockerill show that there is no difference in performance either way. It is generally more feasible to teach beginners to concentrate on the hole, however. Cockerill's study supports the conclusions found by C. R. Griffith in 1928 that blindfolded golfers did as well as those who looked at the ball. (Blind golfers are, in fact, some of the most dedicated of players, as evidenced by the growth of the United States Blind Golfer's Association.)

Sighted golfers nonetheless can make more birdies if they learn to "read the green" accurately. Three major elements affect the ball's path: slope, grain, and the weather as it affects the green.

Determining slope can be tricky. Most players crouch behind the ball and line it up with the cup to see if the ground slopes. It often helps to reverse this exercise and look from the cup to the ball. Other players use their clubs as a plumb-bob: by holding the club perfectly straight above the ball, and using one eye to sight a line to the cup, a player can determine if the hole appears to the left or right of the club, which indicates the ground is sloping in that direction.

Grain, or the direction the grass grows on the green, also influences the roll. The ball goes farther if it is rolling with the grain; slower if against it. Different types of grass also make a difference. The shorter and more tightly bunched the grass, the less influence it will have on the ball's path. If the grass is shiny, it probably means the grain is going away from the player; dull, it is probably toward him.

Water on the green slows a ball down, and also lessens the influence of the grain. If one area of the green is wetter than others, the ball will roll slower through that section.

Of course, a player can avoid the green altogether by shooting a hole-in-one. The key to this strategy, however, is getting the ball in the right hole. Rick Syme, of Macon, Georgia, was recently teeing off on the par-4, 328-yard 17th at Macon's Oak Haven Golf and Country Club. He used a three-wood to cut a corner over the trees, but wind conditions took his fade much farther than planned—clear over to the 16th hole, in fact. Jim Grigsby, who was putting the 16th with his son, had the flagstick out when he heard "Fore!" Syme's ball swished through the trees, landed about seven feet from the hole and rolled in. For this less-than-accurate shot, Syme assessed himself a two-stroke penalty and took a drop off the 16th green. His next shot landed on the 17th green and he one-putted for a bogie 5. Not a bad recovery, Rick.

The Model Golf Swing

Books, magazines, videos, and leading pros all vie to tell golfers how to change their swings for the best hit. The problem is that a swing happens so fast that it's impossible to tell whether the player actually changed his technique or just had good luck. Also, practice in effect only replays the motor program as it exists in the player's head. If that program contains a faulty technique, the practice is a fruitless exercise. Correct performance feedback is essential, which is not available when a player practices alone.

Biomechanics expert Ralph Mann and his associate, PGA professional Fred Griffin, set out to remedy this problem. They developed a video training program that compares a student's swing to a computer-generated model.

Mann developed the computer model after analyzing high-speed pictures taken of fifty-four PGA tour players. This information was fed into a computer and manipulated by Mann to generate "the perfect model swing." The analysis showed that pros tend to be consistent in certain aspects of their play; for example, most of the players place the ball just off the left instep, regardless of the club they use. Mann incorporated this and other similarities into his model. He then personalizes the model for each student at his school, tailoring it to each one's unique physical characteristics.

A videotape is then made of the student's swing, and overlain with the computer model. A comparison immediately provides a clear picture of not only what changes the student should make, but to what degree.

Mann believes that, although the computer is terrific at producing an instructional plan, nothing substitutes for personal training—but training based on the model. Hence, Academy instructors at his school (the Grand Cypress Academy of Golf in Orlando, Florida) personally work with students to ensure that the necessary changes are incorporated into their swings.

Students find some of these changes uncomfortable, and at first may seem to shoot worse than before. Practice pays off, though as they learn excellent golf form, and practice until it becomes second nature.

Chapter 12
Sailing

Wind At Work

"One ship drives east and another drives west
With selfsame winds that blow.
'Tis the set of sails and not the gales
Which tells us the way to go."

—*Ella Wheeler Wilcox*, Winds of Fate

Albert Einstein was a genius where relative motion was concerned, but when he sailed his 14-foot catboat, *Tinif*, he was a lousy sailor. Sailors in the New York area related how each day during the summer of 1939 Einstein would—whatever the weather—"pull back his long, white hair, wrap it in a newspaper, and set out into Peconic Bay." Asked if Einstein knew how to sail, one replied, "There was no external evidence that he did. After pushing *Tinif* off the beach, he mostly drifted around the bay." The professor's head was subject to repeated encounters with the boom, and his boat had to be towed to shore on a regular basis. One day, after capsizing in high winds, Einstein was shown how to reef the sail (i.e., reduce its area). Next day, despite the fact that it was sunny with nary a breeze blowing, he was seen "with the sails shortened as if he were beating into the teeth of a gale." Clearly, his mind was elsewhere.

It may seem to novice sailors that it takes an intellect comparable to Einstein's to learn the specialized vocabulary associated with this sport. The need for precise communication has spawned special words to describe the different type of boats, sails, and maneuvers. Otherwise, a crew member, by just pointing and saying "that way, Captain," is liable to put a boat on the rocks. The parts of a boat discussed in this chapter are illustrated in **Figure 12–1**, though this is hardly a comprehensive picture of what a hard-core sailor knows.

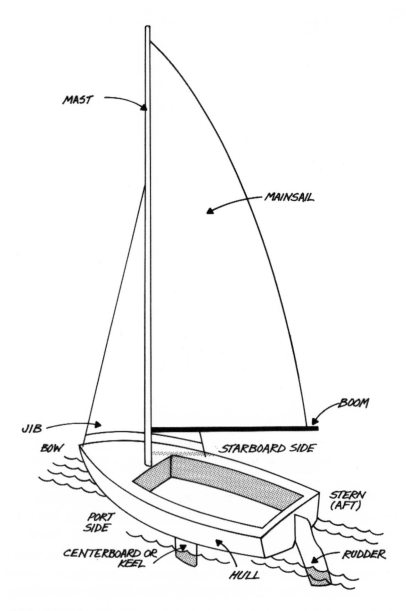

12-1 *Parts of a Boat.*

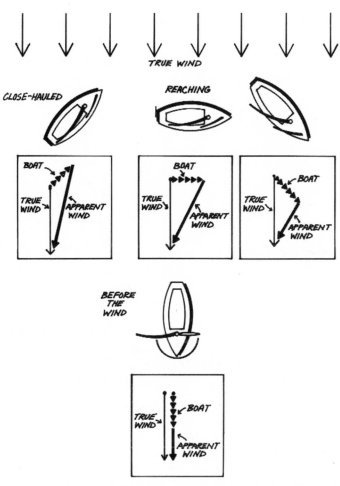

12-2 *True Versus Apparent Wind. When you stand still on land, you feel the true wind, but as soon as you move, that movement causes an apparent change in the wind's direction and speed, called the apparent wind. At sea, a boat's speed and direction determine its apparent wind.*

It is the wind that powers a boat forward. One of the first things a sailor learns, however, is the difference between "true" wind and "apparent" wind **(see Figure 12-2)**. A person standing still on land feels the true wind, but as soon as he or she moves, that movement causes and apparent change in the wind direction and speed. The result of these movements gives rise to the apparent wind. Likewise, a boat's speed and direction determines its apparent wind. It is this wind that the sails "feel," and that drives the boat forward. Sailors string bits of yarn or thread on the rigging to indicate this direction.

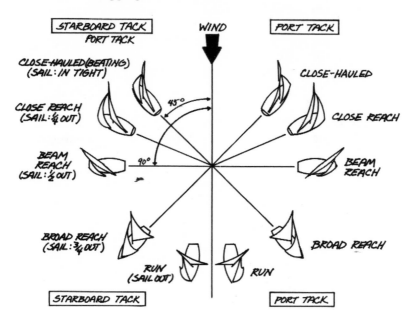

12-3 *Points of Sail. Sailing close-hauled occurs when a sailor takes the boat as close as possible into the face of the wind. Reaching is sailing across the wind. When the boat is running the wind is pushing it from behind. A boat cannot sail directly into the wind because the sails would lose their essential airfoil shape. A sailor must tack (criss-cross) through the wind to make headway.*

Depending on where the sails are set, the apparent wind exerts either a pulling or pushing force: pulling when the boat is reaching or beating, pushing when the boat is running. (These "points of sail" are described in material that follows and depicted in **Figure 12–3**.) When pulling, the sails generate forward motion in much the same manner that an airplane wing generates lift. Because the sail is shaped like an airfoil, the air on the windward side (the side the wind is coming from) moves faster than the air on the leeward side. This increased wind speed causes a corresponding decrease in air pressure on that side (Bernoulli's theorem), leading to a "suction" effect. The faster the air is traveling on both sides of the sail, the more suction, or lift, is created. This suction, in effect, pulls the boat forward **(see Figure 12–4)**.

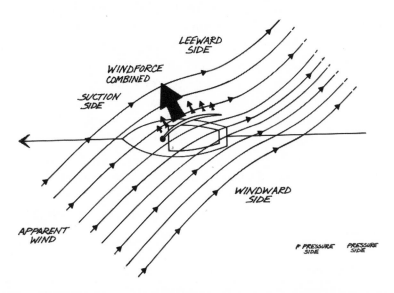

12-4 *Sail Filled with Wind. A sail filled with wind becomes an airfoil, and the air on the windward side (the side the wind is coming from) moves faster than the air on the leeward side. Increased wind speed on the windward side decreases air pressure on that side, leading to a "suction" effect on the leeward side, which pulls the boat forward.*

The resulting wind force, which is actually the sum of many small forces acting on the entire sail, can be represented by a single force representing the total wind magnitude and direction.

One would expect the boat to move in the direction of this arrow, and in all but modern boats, this is the case. Modern hulls, however, not only provide enormous resistance to this leeward drift, but in fact convert a portion of it into forward thrust.

This sideways force is present on all points of sail except downwind running, but especially on a close-hauled tack. It not only causes the boat to move leeward, but to heel over. (A certain amount of heeling, about 30 to 40 degrees, keeps the sails and the tipping force becomes greater than the forward thrust.) When the boat is running downwind, sails no longer act as airfoils but instead as bodies of resistance. Spinnakers are the supreme example; these large, billowing sails are not only functional but are a delight to see.

Most sailboats have a slight "weather helm," meaning that if the helm is left unattended, the boat will tend to head up into the wind until the sails luff (flutter) and the boat stops. This situation is desirable for two reasons: (1) if a gust hits, the boat will somewhat automatically head up and take advantage of the extra speed momentarily available, and (2) if the skipper is single-handling the boat and falls off, the boat will eventually stop itself—although this should never be counted on! Some boats, on the other hand, are so well balanced that the sails can be "trimmed," or set, for a certain course and the helm left virtually unattended, except for periodic minor adjustments. (Racers adjust their sails, continuously, but recreational sailors, particularly if good conversation is underway, often make adjustments only if the sails start luffing or the boat slows down a noticeable amount.)

Points of Sail

Close-Hauled

Sailing close-hauled, also called "beating to windward" or "pointing to windward," occurs when a sailor takes to boat as close as possible into the face of the wind. Under this circumstance, the apparent wind comes from farther ahead than the true wind, and its speed is greater. The faster a sailboat is traveling, the less close it can go to the true wind, because its own apparent wind draws farther and farther ahead.

Modern yachts can sail as close as 45 degrees to the true wind, or about 27 degrees off the apparent wind. Closer than that, and the boat starts "pinching"; the sails luff and, instead of driving the boat forward, the sails act as an air brake. Conversely, if the boat "falls off" the wind too much, the boat begins to stall. The margin between these two points is only two or three degrees, so a sailor looking for top performance must be extremely alert. Stalls can't be seen, but luffs can, so the best way to operate is to stay right under the luff point.

A boat cannot sail directly into the wind because the sails lose their airfoil shape. Hence, if a desired course is in this direction, a sailor must tack, or criss-cross through the wind to make headway. If the wind blows across the starboard (right) side of the boat, it is on a starboard tack; if blowing over the port (left) side, it is on a port tack. (You can remember that port is left by simply recalling that the two words consist of four letters each.) Downwind, if the boom is on the starboard side, the boat is on a port tack, and vice versa.

If the sailor turns the bow of the boat toward and through the wind during tacking, as is normal when beating, the boat is said to come about. Here, the wind shifts from one side of the sail to the other in an easily controlled manner. If he or she turns the bow away from the direction of the wind, it is called jibing. Under this latter circumstance the sails (and boom) can change sides rapidly, which in strong winds can cause a dismasting on larger boats and capsizing on smaller boats.

Reaching

Reaching is sailing across the wind. It is the easiest and fastest point of sail. On a beam reach, the wind is roughly at a right angle to the course line, coming across the beam (side) of the boat. When the wind is slightly forward of the beam, it is a close reach, and when coming aft of the beam, it is a broad, or quartering reach. The sails are let out as far as possible before they luff.

Running

When running, the wind pushes the boat from behind. Sails are let out as far as the rigging allows, with the boom generally at almost a right angle to the centerline of the boat.

Care must be taken that the boat doesn't accidentally jibe. Good sailors develop a keen sense of the wind's direction, in part by sensing it on their necks. In light winds they may wet this area to increase its sensitivity.

To change the direction of the boat, sailors use a tiller or steering wheel. These connect to a rudder that deflects the water. Pulling the tiller to the right makes the bow of the boat swing left, and vice versa.

(A wheel, though, is turned in the direction the sailor wants to go.)

How fast can a sailboat travel? No matter what its size, if it is a displacement boat (i.e., has a keel or a centerboard in place), its maximum speed will depend on its length at the waterline. As the boat moves through the water, it induces a wave as its bow and, except at very slow speeds, one at its stern. The boat's hull, in essence, gets trapped in the trough between these two waves. The maximum length of wave generated is the same as that of the boat's waterline length.

Waves, whether formed under a boat or by wind blowing across the water, have a maximum advancement speed (in knots) of 1.35 times the square root of the wave's length. (See Chapter 15: Surfing.) This factor, 1.235 is the ratio of speed to length. A sailboat can go no faster than the wave it is generating. If a boat measures 40 feet at the waterline, for example, its hull speed cannot exceed 8.54 knots. Because wave resistance increases dramatically as this speed is neared, only in exceptional cases is it actually reached. A more normal speed is two-thirds the maximum, equating to a speed-to-length ratio of 0.90. Oceangoing skippers estimating cruising time do well to use an even lower number, such as 0.75, because ocean waves normally slow a boat down (although in some cases going downwind may increase speed).

Sailboats exceeding their maximum speed for any period of time will disintegrate and sink. Or, as the trough between the waves becomes larger, the freeboard at the fore and aft of the boat decreases and the boat loses the support of water immediately underneath. Ultimately, the boat literally sails under the wave and sinks. Many of the old square-riggers lost at sea may have met their demise this way, if the crew couldn't lower the sails quickly enough when a storm hit.

Nonballasted dinghies and multihull boats can get around the wave problem by "planing," and achieve terrific speeds as a result. When a boat planes, it mounts its own bow wave and rides it, and leaves the stern wave behind. To plane, a boat must be lightweight and have a hull that is flat in the aft section. It must also have a squared-off stern so that the flow of water "detaches," rather than being carried along with the boat. Boats having these characteristics will plane when they reach a speed-to-length ratio of about 1.78. (At ratios between 1.5 and 1.6, a boat is in a danger zone, as previously described, and between 1.6 and 1.78, the boat "surfs.")

Planing allows a boat to go as fast as, and sometimes exceed, the speed of the true wind. Displacement yachts, on the other hand, can normally go only about half as fast.

Most modern sailboats have either one or two masts. The following common varieties exist of each.

On single-masted boats:

A catboat has one sail, placed well forward.

A sloop has one foresail.

A cutter has two or three foresails.

A classic cutter has two foresails and one or two topsails.

On two-masted boats:

A yawl has a small mast (mizzen), located aft of the rudder.

A ketch has a larger mizzen mast located forward of the waterline.

A schooner has an aft mast that is taller than the forward mast (the former being the main mast). Some schooners have three masts (in which case the after mast isn't necessarily the tallest). Schooners do not perform well to windward, so have lost favor in recent decades.

A staysail schooner has a triangular staysail and a fore topsail.

Except on certain classes of racing boats, most sailors of larger boats prefer two masts because the sails are smaller and therefore easier to handle. For effective forward thrust per unit of sail area, though, one mast is more effective, and is preferred for racing **(see Figure 12–5)**.

All of the boats previously described are monohulls and have keels (or centerboards) that provide resistance to capsizing. The boats are designed, in fact, so that if a certain heeling angle is reached, they will automatically start righting themselves. Or if they do go over, the weight distribution brings them back up again.

Multihulls, whether catamarans or trimarans, receive their stability from having a very wide beam and by having two or three centers of buoyancy. These boats have always had to fight for respect, and many

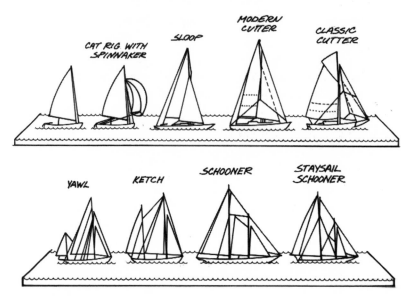

12-5 *Sail Rigs. Single-masted boats (top) give more effective forward thrust per unit of sail area than boats with two masts, and are preferred for racing. Two-masted rigs (bottom) are preferred by most sailors of larger boats because the sails are smaller and therefore easier to handle.*

old salts shun them. However, multihulls are quite popular in Europe, and the United States is seeing ever more converts, especially among sailors interested in speed. A 16-foot Hobie Cat (catamaran) can fly across the water at 20 knots—much faster than most keeled day sailors, which are lucky to muster seven knots.

The trouble with multihulls is that if they capsize, it is virtually impossible for the crew to right them. This is the principal reason some traditional sailors avoid using them for cruising. However, a monohull in trouble may sink, whereas a multihull will, under most conditions, stay afloat—albeit perhaps upside down—making the vessel quite a reliable lifeboat.

One definite negative of monohulls is their propensity for rolling side to side on downwind tacks. Because most long-distance cruises favor this point of sail, serious discomfort can result. Sailors frustrated with spilled coffee and cocktails, and weary of buttocks made sore from sliding across a wet cockpit, may find a multihull's flat ride particularly refreshing.

Weather Forecasting and Navigation

Two skills necessary for cruising the high seas are weather forecasting and navigation. Modern boats often carry sophisticated instruments that handle these tasks, but all sailors should still have a rudimentary knowledge of the subjects in case of equipment failure. To that end, the following adages are good to memorize, not only be sea-going sailors but, for that matter, landlubbers who may be lost in a forest for desert.

Weather Clues
- This old saying is surprisingly accurate: "Red sky at night, sailor's delight. Red sky in the morning, sailor take warning." Also, a bright yellow sunset indicates wind; pale green indicates rain.
- For storms, "Long foretold, long last; short warning, soon past."
- In the northern hemisphere, weather usually moves from west to east. The weather currently 400 to 500 miles west is the weather here tomorrow.
- Clouds building into an anvil shape indicate a storm within an hour.
- Clouds showing "mare's tails" with little motion indicates gales from the direction the tail radiates.
- A halo around the moon indicates rain within twelve hours.
- If the wind blows strongly before it rains, expect a short storm; rain before wind, a longer storm.
- If after a storm the weather improves too rapidly, expect another low to move in.
- Static on low-frequency AM stations indicates an approaching lightning storm.
- In the summer: Quickly rising temperatures indicate good weather.
- In the winter: Quickly rising temperatures indicate bad weather.
- The presence of porpoises in shallow water indicates bad weather on its way.

Navigation

To estimate the speed of a boat, drop a wad of paper at the bow and time how long it takes to get to the stern. Then, use the following formulas.

Boat speed in knots: $\dfrac{\text{Time in seconds}}{\text{Length}}$ x 0.59

Boat speed in mph: $\dfrac{\text{Time in seconds}}{\text{Length}}$ x 0.68

The reason mariners use knots instead of miles per hour is that nautical miles relate directly to degrees of latitude. One degree of latitude equals 60 nautical miles, and one nautical mile equals one second. Because charts always describe a position in terms of latitude and longitude, no conversion is necessary. (One degree of longitude varies with the latitude, however, from 60 miles at the equator to zero at the poles.) One knot equals 6,076 feet per hour, or about 1.15 mph.

If you become lost, the following are useful tips:

- Orient yourself so that the hour hand on your watch is directed at the sun. (If you have a digital watch, draw a clock face on a piece of paper or in the dirt, with the hour hand pointing at the sun.) South lies halfway between this direction and 12 o'clock. (Always go in a direction toward noon; that is, clockwise before noon, counterclockwise after noon.)
- Make a fist and fully extend your arm. The width of four knuckles is about 10 degrees (with thumb extended, about 15 degrees).
- At night, find north by locating Polaris (the North Star). It is the star at the end of the Little Dipper's handle. The easiest way to locate it is by looking upward from the Big Dipper. The elevation of Polaris (in degrees) will also approximate your latitude.

Sand and Ice Sailing

Henry Beard and Roy McKie describe an iceboat in their book *Sailing*: "A sailboat having such characteristics that it is statistically more likely to crash than to sink; that it can become a total loss without sinking; and that in the event of mishap, its crew will be able to walk to shore."

In the event of a mishap, however, the boat will probably be going exceedingly fast. Because these "boats" do not contend with wave formation and water resistance, dramatically high speeds are possible—up to three or more times that of the true wind. You'll never see these vehicles with spinnakers; resistance-type sails only slow them down. Instead, the boats tack downwind, a marvel in itself.

Speeds of 115 mph have been recorded for ice yachts, when the wind was blowing less than 30 mph. (The record is 143 mph, achieved by John D. Buckstaff of Wisconsin in 1938.)

Ice yachts are typically cat-rigged; that is, they carry only one sail. Also, they can't be sailed close to the wind or they slow down. Whereas a conventional yacht points about 45 degrees off the true wind, and a catamaran about 56 degrees, an ice yacht shouldn't venture any closer than 67 degrees. (Because of their high speed, the apparent wind moves forward so that even 67 degrees is "close-hauled," in a sense.)

Ice boating was notably popular in the nineteenth century, particularly on the Hudson River in New York, which would freeze for a distance of about 100 miles upstream from the mouth. Commodore John A. Roosevelt built the largest recorded iceboat, *Icicle*, in 1869. The yacht was almost 69 feet long.

Sand yachts are not as fast as their brothers on ice, partly because of the friction between the tires and the sand. They travel "only" at about 60 to 80 mph. One of the difficulties encountered by these skippers is finding long stretches of hard, sandy beaches.

Sand boats are easily built; however, they must be sturdy to withstand the high stresses put on them (greater than those experienced by water yachts). Most have two rear wheels and a single front wheel. Skippers wear seatbelts, goggles, and helmets, and the boats typically include rollbars.

Rigid wings similar to those on the Walker Planesail have also been adapted to land yachting by Philip and Art Rothrock of Portland, Oregon. Their boat, *Bliss*, takes advantages of a NASA aircraft wing design that uses a single-slotted, three-element airfoil with one flap. The Rothrocks are now cruising dry lake beds and desert floors at 85 mph.

By using cams, and bicycle chains and sprockets, they can rotate the entire wing or just the angle of the flap. The wing consists of birch plywood skin over wooden ribs, with a leading edge made of foam.

Boardsailers, frustrated by short summer seasons, are adapting their equipment for winter use. They add blades for ice sailing; skis for snow sailing.

A variation on ice and sand sailing is railroad-car sailing. Years ago the Kansas Pacific Railroad made repairs to its lines from such "vessels." These sailing cars averaged 30 mph.

Chapter 13
Skiing

The Downhill Thrill

"The basic pleasures of downhill skiing are primitive—speed, accomplishment, the pleasures of smoothness and rhythm, and the tingle of fear and the exhilaration in overcoming it."
　　　　　　　　　　　　　—Mark Heller, From The Skier's Encyclopedia

Skis have come a long way since "Snowshoe" John A. Thompson carried the mail over the Sierra Nevada Mountains in the 1850s. The first well-known skier in the United States, Thompson somehow managed the 90-mile route from Placerville to Carson Valley on 11-foot homemade oak skis. He hadn't invented anything new, however; Europeans' fondness for wooden skis had existed for more than a thousand years.

Thompson wouldn't recognize the sleek, short skis in use today, and he would be amazed at the easy way skiers carve quick turns in the powder he so laboriously plowed.

Ski manufacturers tailor their products for specific types of skiing. The most general divisions are Nordic and Alpine skiing. Nordic includes cross-country skiing, cross-country touring, and ski jumping. Alpine includes slalom, giant slalom, downhill racing, alpine touring, ski mountaineering, and freestyle skiing.

In cross-country Nordic races, courses are as natural as possible, often through the woods. Roughly one-third of the course is uphill, one-third downhill, and one-third flat. These skiers achieve average speeds of 12 mph, compared to an average of 60 mph for Alpine racers.

Nordic courses have a maximum height difference set over the entire course; alpine courses have minimum and maximum vertical drop. **Table 13–I** lists these parameters by event.

Table 13-1
Course Lengths for Nordic and Alpine Events

NORDIC EVENTS

CATEGORY	DESCRIPTION	MAXIMUM HEIGHT DIFFERENCE OVER COURSE
Women's events	5 km (3.1 mi)	100 m (109 yd)
	4 x 5 km (3.1 mi) relay	100 m (109 yd)
	10 km (6.2 mi)	150 m (164 yd)
Men's events	4 x 10 km (6.2 mi) relay	200 m (219 yd)
	15 km (9.3 mi)	250 m (273 yd)
	30 km (18.6 mi)	250 m (273 yd)
	50 km (31 mi)	250 m (273 yd)

ALPINE EVENTS

EVENT	VERTICAL DROP
Men's downhill	800-1000 m (875-1094 yd)
Women's downhill	500-700 m (547-766 yd)
Men's giant slalom	250-400 m (273-437 yd)
Women's giant slalom	250-350 m (273-383 yd)
Men's slalom	180-220 m (197-241 yd)
Women's slalom	130-180 m (142-197 yd)
Parallel slalom	80-100 m (88-109 yd)

Downhill races have few turns and are the fastest type of race. Slalom courses twist and turn, and giant slalom courses include both downhill and slalom elements. Except for the parallel slalom, these races are against the clock; in the parallel slalom, two skiers race against each other down a parallel course.

Turning is a main element of modern skiing, and to that end manufacturers put most of their research-and-development efforts into this aspect. Speed is less important. (In fact, some of the old wooden boards used in the 1800s were faster than today's sleek, plastic models—but the skier couldn't turn.)

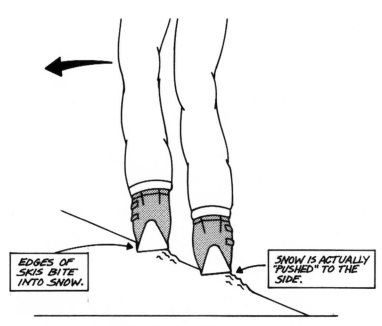

EDGES OF
SKIS BITE
INTO SNOW.

SNOW IS ACTUALLY
"PUSHED" TO THE
SIDE.

13-1   *How the Edge of Skis Bite into Snow. Because ski boots form a solid connection between ski and knee, a slight lateral motion of the knees causes the skis' edges to bite into the snow.*

A skier turns either by shifting weight or by rotating the body. As modern skis have become more controllable, more of the lower body is used. As a skier shifts his weight from one ski to the other, his center of gravity also shifts, which affects his speed and direction. In the past, students began with a snow plow and worked up to a parallel turn; today they begin with the parallel turn. Because ski boots form a solid connection between ski and knee, with no sideways movement allowed, a slight lateral motion of the knees causes the edges to bite into the snow **(see Figure 13–1)**.

Modern boots, with all of their benefits, have one major drawback: they make knees very vulnerable to injury. The boots come so far up the leg that the strain of twists and shocks transfers directly to the knee. A study covering two decades of skiing injuries in northern Vermont shows that the odds of a skier suffering knee damage are nearly three times greater now than in the early seventies. By contrast, the odds of breaking a leg have decreased by 90 percent, but a broken leg is likely to be less serious than a knee injury because knee problems often require complicated surgery and a long rehabilitation process.

Records being set in speed skiing, an event first recognized by the International Ski Federation in 1965, are making this specialized area of skiing ever more dangerous. The current record is 155.434 mph set by Frenchman Phillippe Goitschel at Les Arcs, France, in 2002. Skiers in this event fine tune every aspect of the downhill run. A perfect aerodynamic posture, specially designed helmets, and ski poles contoured to the skier's body all contribute to the extraordinary velocities achieved by these skiers.

Figure 13–2 shows the forces acting on a speeding downhill racer.

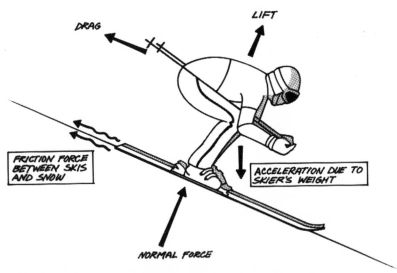

13-2   *Forces Acting on a Speeding Downhill Racer. Although computer models have calculated drag coefficient and other aerodynamics forces, all of the data generated so far can contribute only to theory until more wind tunnel testing is done.*

As a skier's speed increases, so does the work required to keep the legs in the right position, because the force acting on the legs is directed outward. The velocity of air is greater around the torso than between the skier's legs so a decrease of air pressure occurs between the skier's thighs. This pressure difference tends to pull the skier's knees together, which in turn causes a change in the angle of attack of the skier's legs,

a. a. SIDE VIEW.

THICKEST POINT OF SKI

TAIL	AFTERBODY	WAIST	FOREBODY	SHOVEL

b. BOTTOM SURFACE.

HEEL- (SECOND WIDEST POINT)	WAIST (NARROWEST POINT)	SHOULDER- (WIDEST POINT)

13-3 *Anatomy of a Ski. Skis are wider in the front and back than in the middle. The degree of this curve is called the sidecut. At top (a) is a ski seen from the side. Below (b), the ski's bottom surface.*

and the legs slip away from each other. Too great a change of attack, and the skier is likely to lose control. The greater the speed, the more acute this problem becomes.

How a ski responds to a skier's movement and to the slope depends on various factors, with the ski's shape and composition being especially important. Buyers of new skis have a huge selection to choose from (about 400 models). Because the boards are so closely tailored to different skiing demands, a new skier should buy from a professional who knows the differences among the models.

Skis are slightly wider in the front and back than in the middle. The degree of this curve, called sidecut, determines the radius of curvature the skier experiences when the edge is pressed against the snow (see **Figure 13-3**). The smaller the radius, the sharper the turn. Also, the shorter the ski, the more responsive it is to this pressure, so beginning skiers often start out with shorter skis.

A ski tail (the back end of a ski) can be either soft or hard. A soft tail makes turning easier; a stiff one keeps the ski straight, a condition more suitable for downhill racing. Freestyle skis, used in a ballet skiing, have a slightly upturned tail to facilitate backward skiing.

Steel edges increase the grip on the snow and promote quicker turns, but they are a major cause of vibration. Edges are either solid from tip to toe (tension edge), or are segmented (cracked). Cracked edges have metal strips that are hinged together. This arrangement increases a ski's flexibility.

Ultra-slippery polyethylene plastic is the base material used in most skis. This material is so slick that the skis of a downhill racer moving at 70 mph will create only 13 pounds of drag. (Wind resistance, on the other hand, generates between 18 and 80 pounds, depending on the skier's stance.) Bases differ in the quality of plastic used, which is defined primarily by the size of the molecules. A longer molecule makes for a tougher and faster ride. Low-quality bases may have molecule lengths of 1 million atoms; high-quality ones vary from 2 to 10 million. The latter material is more porous, so it takes wax better.

Skis also use different patterns of grooves in the base to help remove melted snow. Friction between the base and snow crystals creates heat, which partially melts the crystals. The resulting film of water must be

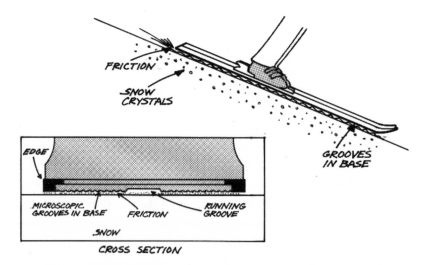

13-4 *Friction When Ski Meets Snow. Friction between the ski base and snow crystals creates heat, which partially melts the crystals. The microscopic grooves in the base control and channel this film of water.*

just the right thickness or the ski slows down. The microscopic grooves in the base control and channel this film of water **(see Figure 13–4)**. Some of the newest skis have split bases that feature harder material under the tip (shovel) and softer material in the center and tail. Wax also helps the water and ice layer to shear away from the bottom of the ski.

As skis have gotten stronger, the tips curve up to a lesser degree than did earlier skis. Older skis, particularly those made from wood, had large tips, presumably to keep the ski from breaking. This design was of questionable efficacy, though, in that skis still broke. Smaller tips reduce swing weight and so allow easier turning. Glide characteristics also improve. Some newer models of skis even have removable tips, so a skier can install specific sizes to suit the snow condition.

Skiers worldwide can thank Howard Head for making the first major improvement in snow skis. A ski school instructor once told him, "If men were meant to ski on metal skis, God would have made trees out of metal." Head's background as an aircraft engineer made him skeptical of this advice and he set out in 1947 to prove the instructor wrong. It took three years to develop a marketable product, but the result was an aluminum ski laminated to a wood core, or a so-called metal sandwich ski. His invention revolutionized the sport. According to Head, "Lightness is not what makes a ski better," although he originally thought it would. "In trying to build a light ski, I accidentally produced a ski that was stiffer in torsion, one that would turn and track more easily. That was the magic difference." (Head had a gift for fortuity, it seems; his second famous "accident"—the oversized racket—revolutionized the game of tennis.)

During this development period, Head's employees were so loyal that they worked for him without pay for a year. But it was worth it: Head's skis were three times more flexible than their wood predecessors, and for the first time in history of skiing, turning was made easy. By adjusting torsional and flexion characteristics, Head was also able to shorten the skis by up to 15 inches. (The Fischer Company of Austria is also credited with this design change.) A reduction in length reduces the rotational forces required to turn the ski, making this maneuver easier. Short skis were used before this time, but they did not work well.

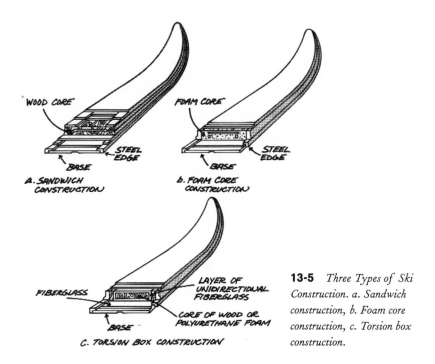

13-5 *Three Types of Ski Construction. a. Sandwich construction, b. Foam core construction, c. Torsion box construction.*

Throughout the fifties and sixties, Head continued making improvements, including the damping of vibrations that can knock a skier out of control. Between 1947 and 1970, the years he owned his company, the number of skiers worldwide increased from 50,000 to more than 4 million (and has since increased to over 45 million). Head's skis made the sport easier to learn and more fun, and thus contributed to this growth.

The next major improvement in skis came in the late sixties, with torsion-box, or wet-wrap, construction. Here, a core of either wood or a polyurethane foam with a layer of unidirectional fiberglass is put on top of a light sheet of fiberglass, with the entire structure wrapped in a "sock" of epoxy. The ski is compressed at about 150 pounds per square inch in a steel mold and "cooked" at 210 to 300° F **(see Figure 13-5)**.

Fischer skis vary this procedure with a patented process called Vacuum Technic. The ski layers are dry when put in the mold, then the air is pumped out and resin injected with a precisely metered, computer-controlled injector system. The vacuum condition causes the resin to be evenly distributed throughout the structure. This process reportedly produces a stronger, more consistent ski. The heating process takes place at lower temperatures, which is also better for the materials.

The composition of all modern skis includes some fiberglass-reinforced plastic, either by a wet-wrap, lamination, or Vacuum Technic process. Fiberglass and epoxy make a natural damper, and can flex a considerable amount without breaking. At least sixteen ski manufacturers now include a layer of DuPont's Kevlar 49, a polyaramid fiber that effectively damps high vibrations. On a Kevlar slalom ski, Kevlar makes up about 25 percent of the ski, by volume; in giant slalom skis, slightly less. Carbon fibers (graphite) are also added to some skis to increase strength and stiffness. These fibers, which also act as a damper, run longitudinally down the ski.

Many skis sandwich the fiberglass layers between aluminum strips. Besides providing stiffness and strength, these strips increase flexibility, much as a leaf spring does on a car. Because aluminum can permanently bend when riding over a bump, it is usually not used in soft skis or where moguls (large bumps) are anticipated.

Cores are made of wood, foam, or plastic. The core material determines the flex pattern of the ski, and affects the total weight. Typical woods include beech, spruce, and ash. A foam core uses polyurethane foam, which can be given different densities according to the characteristics desired—a harder material for a stiffer ride, for example.

A tough plastic coats the top and sides of the skis. This material protects the inside layers—and lets manufacturers embed striking patterns and logos in it.

In the 1990's, a big innovation in skis was the cap design. Cap skis use a single sheet of material to form the top and sidewalls. Because the cap structurally replaces some layers of the skis, weight is reduced. Initially, only three companies manufactured true cap skis: Elan, Volant, and Saloman. Volant uses stainless steel for its cap. Other companies have followed with a similar design, but instead of replacing layers they simply put a seamless sheath over the ski. Each design gives an entirely different response: caps are extremely fast and "alive"; sheaths are smoother, but slower.

A ski's flexibility depends on its camber, that is, the strength of its arch. The components used, as well as the thickness of the core and the degree of sidecut, influence this strength. A thinner core rides more softly. When a skier hits a bump, the skis flex and the skier is actually lifted into the air, although the skis may not leave the ground. Expert skiers generally prefer a stiffer ski because it is more responsive at high speeds.

All ski manufacturers tout vibration control as a main selling point of their products. As a skier races down a slope, the skis experience both low and high vibrations, just as guitar or piano strings do. Generally, the greater the speed, the higher the frequency of vibrations. The skier's legs absorb those in the lower ranges, from 10 to 50 Hz (hertz), but those between 50 and 300 Hz can shake the skis out of control. (One hertz equals a frequency of one cycle per second.) It is this upper range that manufacturers try to dampen. A damped ski provides a smoother ride, and because the ski doesn't bounce around so much, better edge grip is maintained.

Snow itself acts as a good damper, but when hard or icy terrain is encountered, additional internal damping cushions the ride. Too much damping, though, causes skis to feel dead on soft snow. Also, a certain amount of vibration is necessary to keep melted snow from building up on the base.

Manufacturers damp skis in a variety of ways. Layering in itself encourages damping, because the internal movement of the layers absorbs vibration. The addition of Kevlar in some skis not only lessens the weight and increases the strength, but effectively damps high-frequency vibrations. Maurice Woehrle, technical advisor for the Rossignol ski company, says that Kevlar improves the edge grip, making the ski more stable and efficient, and that without Kevlar, "the snow always feels harder."

Fear is part of the experience of skiing, and both novices and experts grapple with overcoming it. Fear tightens muscles and makes a skier more susceptible to injury. If the hips and knees are overly tense, instead of acting as shock absorbers they remain compressed, unable to react to differences in terrain. Timothy Gallwey and Bob Kriegel, in

Inner Skiing, suggest various ways to confront and overcome this fear. They show how relaxed concentration, trusting one's body, and quieting the conscious mind not only improve one's skiing techniques, but vastly increase the enjoyment as well.

Still, some fear is a good thing if it serves to prevent the skier from speeding out of control. People do die in skiing accidents, primarily from high-speed collisions with stationary objects. According to Paul L. Morrow, MD, chief investigator in an ongoing study of Vermont skiing fatalities, "Uncontrolled speed appears to be the most prevalent lethal factor." Out of 22 fatalities that occurred in this area between 1979 and 1988 (nine seasons), 18 were from head injuries. In 17 cases, skiers collided with stationary objects (12 trees, 2 rocks, 2 lift towers, and 1 drainage ditch). Only two of the deaths were attributable to falls on slopes rated above the skier's ability. Overall, however, the risk of the sport is low. In this study, there was one death per 1.6 million skier days.

Recreational skiers who are put off by cold weather, despite the availability of thermal socks and battery-operated hand warmers, might wish to try grass skiing. The boards for this sport are shorter than snow skis, and are moved down the slopes by rollers or caterpillar tracks. Instead of ice burns, a skier need only worry about grass burns . . . and avalanches are unknown.

Extreme Skiing

One activity that deliberately courts disaster is extreme skiing. Chris Landry, an American who has skied Pyramid Peak in Colorado, Mount Rainier in Washington, Mount McKinley in Alaska, and the Mendel Couloir in the Sierra Nevadas, puts it bluntly: "The definition of extreme skiing is pretty simple—if you fall, you die."

These skiers tackle slopes that have 50 or more degrees of pitch, giving true meaning to the term fall line. (Few of the steepest expert runs at U.S. ski areas exceed 30 degrees of pitch.) On Landry's trip down Pyramid Peak, in some places he could make only four or five slow turns before the sloughing snow set loose by his ski edges threatened to knock him down.

Sylvain Saudan, a Swiss ski instructor, is considered the pioneer of extreme skiing. He has skied down many "unskiable" mountains, and set a record for steepest descent when, in 1967, he skied the north face of the Aiguille de Bionnassay, a 13,937-foot peak in the French Alps. With an average steepness of 55 to 60 degrees, it is rated as the steepest and iciest of the Alpine peaks. Says Saudan: "I love danger, and I love mountains! . . . I take these extreme steep slopes for personal satisfaction. After all, we must all try to achieve something in life." Unfortunately, a few extremists have achieved their deaths, instead.

Landry is one of the few Americans who have engaged in the European style of extreme skiing. More prevalent in America is an attitude of "court risk, but not death." Getting down the chutes and cliffs of Squaw Valley qualifies. Tough, but not deadly. Avalanches pose a larger threat than does falling. Manufacturers who sell skis in the U.S. which they label "extreme" have Squaw Valley, not Mount Everest, in mind.

Chapter 14
Skydiving

Free-Falling From the Skies

"If the good Lord had wanted man to stay on the ground, He would have given us roots."

—*Dan Poynter, From* Parachuting: The Skydiver's Handbook

High-risk sports: Why does a person put his or her life on the line just for a quick thrill? This is a question frequently asked participants in skydiving, bungee jumping, and aerobatic flying. Not long ago, psychiatrists blamed Freudian death wishes or the participant's urge to make up for feeling of inadequacy. Studies have consistently shown that this theory is wrong, but old beliefs die hard.

For example, in 1973, Bruce Ogilvie studied 293 high-risk competitors and found them to be success-oriented, strongly extroverted, above average in abstract ability, and superior in intelligence—but not crazy. In fact, only 6 percent of the subjects studied competed in high-risk sports because they felt angry or because they felt inadequate. Ogilvie believes that risk takers have a strong "go for it" attitude coupled with a belief that they can only learn by doing.

To these adventurers, the threat of possible loss of life is not as great as the risk of not living—and they perceive a great difference between the two. Risk takers are generally not reckless; they participate in their chosen sports only after a cool and calculated assessment of the danger involved.

Skydiving is certainly a sport that appeals to risk takers—about 110,000 of them in North America. Improvements made in the last twenty years, though, particularly in equipment, have made the sport much safer, so the risk has significantly decreased. Actually, the sport has a relatively low fatality rate: about one in 75,000 jumps. More than 2 million jumps are taken in the United States every year, with fewer than thirty fatalities. Many more people die each year from scuba diving or bicycle accidents.

Whether a jumper is making their first or thousandth jump, the process consists of four stages: going up, free-falling, the canopy ride, and the landing.

Going Up

For students, the heights from which the initial jumps occur depend on where they are on their training schedule, and on whether they are learning with a static line or by accelerated free-fall (AFF). On a static line jump, the parachute is deployed by a line attached to the aircraft. Generally, students learning by this method must make five jumps using the static line before they can jump without it, and they make a total of fifteen jumps before qualifying for a 60-second free-fall.

Table 14–1 shows a typical jump schedule for static-line training.

	Table 14–1	
	Jump Schedule for Static-Line Training	
JUMP NUMBERS	DESCRIPTION	JUMPER'S STARTING ALTITUDE (FEET ABOVE GROUND LEVEL)
1, 2	Basic orientation (on static line)	2,800
3, 4, 5	Practice rip cord pulls (on static line)	2,800
6	Jump and pull	3,200
7, 8	10-second delay	4,000
9, 10	15-second delay	5,000
11, 12	30-second delay	7,500
13, 14, 15	45-second delay	9,500

A jumper is now qualified for a 60 second delayed drop. AFF training enables a student to progress much faster. It requires that two certified (AFF-rated) instructors accompany the student both during the exit from the plane and during free-fall for the first three jumps. On jumps four through seven, one instructor goes along. These instructors are intimately familiar with the aerodynamic positions they must take in order to remain in touching distance, so that they can pull the student's rip cord if necessary. The primary advantage of AFF training is that a jumper needs only seven jumps to qualify for unsupervised parachuting, compared with fifteen for static-line training. Also, the first jump is made from 9,000 feet, with both students and instructor free-falling to the 4,000-foot level. The United States Parachute Association (USPA) approved the AFF training program in 1981.

Tandem jumps are sometimes substituted for static-line jumps. Or, for a person just wanting to jump once, tandem jumping can be the way to go. After only a brief checkout, students can head to the skies with their instructor. Typically, they'll jump from 5,000 feet or higher and experience true free-fall conditions. Special equipment is used, including a bigger chute (390 to 425 square feet, compared with 250 square feet for a regular chute) and a special harness, which is snapped to the instructor's.

The Free-Fall

After jumping from the airplane, gravity quickly causes a diver's speed to accelerate to about 110 mph. As this speed increases, however, so does the resisting force of air. After about 9 to 12 seconds, or about 1,500 feet, the upward force of the air is equal to the gravitational force pulling downward (i.e., drag force is equal to weight), and the fall from that point on (until the canopy opens) is at a constant speed. This limiting factor on speed, called terminal velocity, is the reason a raindrop, after falling from perhaps 4,000 feet, doesn't strike your head at 245 mph, which it would otherwise do in the absence of air resistance. Because of their small size and weight, raindrops have a terminal velocity of about 15 mph—fortunately, or it wouldn't be safe to go outside when it was raining.

By assuming different positions during free-fall, sky divers can increase or decrease the amount of air resistance their bodies are subject to, and thereby increase or decrease their terminal velocity **(see Figure 14–1).**

THE SCIENCE OF SPORTS

THE SCIENCE OF SPORTS

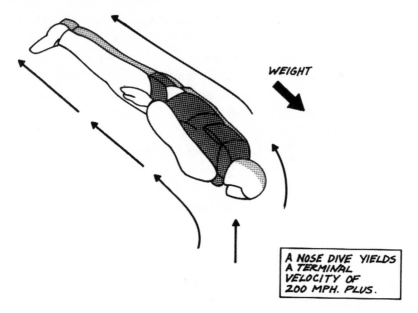

WEIGHT

A NOSE DIVE YIELDS A TERMINAL VELOCITY OF 200 MPH. PLUS.

14-1 *Dive Positions. By assuming different positions during free-fall, skydivers can alter the amount of air resistance encountered by their bodies, and thereby increase or decrease their terminal velocity. A nose dive yields a terminal velocity of more than 200 mph.*

Moments after jumping from a DC-4 near Coolidge, Arizona, Gregory Robertson saw fellow parachutist Debbie Williams collide with another diver, knocking her unconscious. Robertson was 40 feet above them at the time, in a "spread eagle" position, which has a terminal velocity of 100–120 mph **(see Figure 14-2)**. He quickly assumed a "no-lift" dive position, which almost instantly increased his speed to 200 mph. At 3,500 feet, he caught up to Williams and, after positioning her so that her chute would open easily, yanked her rip cord just 10 seconds before impact. The 7,000-foot chase had taken 25 seconds. Although Williams suffered a skull fracture, nine broken ribs, and a perforated kidney (some of which may have occurred during the landing, because she landed on her back), she was lucky to be alive. The other diver in the collision, Guy Fitzwater, suffered a broken leg. There is no record of any other successful rescue of this nature in recreational skydiving, although several other attempts ended with both divers crashing to the

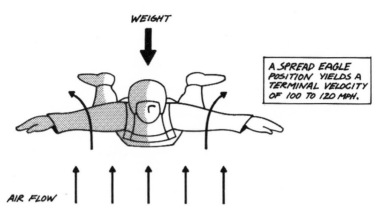

14-2   *Spread Eagle Position. This position yields a terminal velocity of 100 to 120 mph.*

ground—cratering in chute parlance. Robertson subsequently was granted a record in the *Guinness Book of World Records* for "lowest midair rescue."

The higher up one is in the sky, the less air resistance encountered. At 19 miles up, the air is very thin indeed, as Air Force Captain Joseph Kittinger can attest. In 1960, he jumped from a balloon at 102,000 feet, achieving a breathtaking terminal velocity of 614 mph (or 702—depending on which report you read). Either way, he was at almost supersonic speed—the speed of sound being 740 mph. Kittinger was in free-fall for 4.5 minutes (a small stabilizing chute was worn to control rotation) for a distance of 84,700 feet, or 16 miles, and the total jump lasted almost 14 minutes. The jump put him in Guinness for "longest delayed drop." (Kittinger was also the first person to solo across the Atlantic in a helium balloon. The 1984 trip took him from Maine to Italy.)

Conditions at extreme altitudes are hazardous; Kittinger's normal weight of 150 pounds doubled to 300 pounds with the addition of survival equipment, including a pressurized space suit. At 102,800 feet, though, he weighed 3 pounds less—gravity decreases 1 percent for each 100,000 feet of altitude.

Seasoned sky divers liken free-fall to flying, rather than falling, especially once they reach terminal velocity. Air resistance provides a medium against which to make turns, loops, and rolls. Divers must control their positions, though, or they may go into uncontrolled rolls and spins. Use of the spread-eagle position helps control this danger.

The Canopy Ride

At about 2,500 feet, a sky diver deploys his chute, which typically has a diameter of about 28 feet. Air resistance immediately increases tenfold, and the terminal velocity proportionately decreases, to about ten feet per second, or 7mph. The forces acting on an open chute are drag, lift, relative wind, pressurized air, and the jumper's suspended weight **(see Figure 14–3)**.

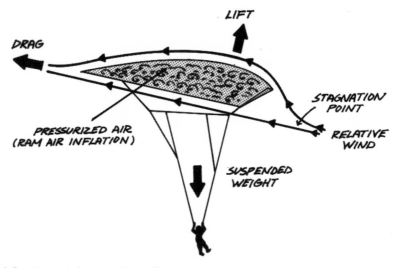

14-3 *Forces Acting on an Open Chute.*

The USPA now requires that all AFF students carry an automatic activation device (AAD), which automatically initiates the chute's opening at a preset altitude if a certain speed is exceeded. (The latter criterion is important; otherwise, the device would activate even if the student had already pulled the rip cord. Although this activation shouldn't cause danger to the parachutist, it is not particularly good for the device.) Steve Snyder invented the Sentinel automatic opener in 1960, and for twenty-seven years the device saved many lives. The invention

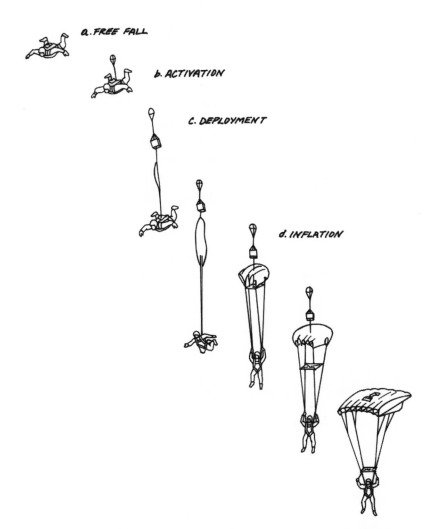

a. FREE FALL

b. ACTIVATION

c. DEPLOYMENT

d. INFLATION

14-4 *Ram-Air Deployment Inflation Sequence. (a.) Free-fall is just what it says until the point (b. activation) when the diver pulls a ripcord to release the pilot chute container or hand releases the pilot chute. (c.) Deployment: the pilot chute encounters drag and "anchors" itself in the jumper's air stream. The ensuing tension on the connecting line pulls the main chute from its container, and then pulls the chute out of the bag. (d.) Inflation: inflated with pressurized air, the parachute's "cells" create a semi-rigid wing with upper and lower surfaces and an airfoil section. The wind blows into the open end and pumps the chute up like a balloon.*

also won him the Leo Stevens medal, parachuting's highest honor. Unfortunately, product liability considerations prompted him to withdraw it from the market in 1987.

Some experienced sky divers do not carry an AAD, both because of the rather high cost and because they are leery of premature or accidental release. (Yet, the USPA says that they have never received a report of a sky diver dying from an AAD accidentally going off. They do have, however, many reports from people who say the device saved their lives.) Some sky divers prefer using an audio altimeter, which beeps at a preselected altitude. Also developed by Snyder, this device is especially useful in "relative work," where two or more sky divers form a star or other formation.

It takes about three seconds for a parachute to fully deploy. The following three steps are involved **(see Figure 14–4)**:

Activation
The chute container is released by either pulling a rip cord or by hand-releasing a pilot chute.

Deployment
The pilot chute, a small chute about 34 inches in diameter, encounters drag and "anchors" itself in the jumper's air stream. The ensuing tension on the connecting line effectively pulls the main chute bag from its container, and then pulls the chute out of the bag. Modern chutes use deployment devices, such as sleeves or "diapers," which increase the reliability of the opening by keeping the lines separate and under an even load.

Inflation
The most common type of parachute used today is the rectangular-shaped ram-air canopy (although many chutists call it square). In many ways it works like a solid aircraft wing. The parachute consists of two layers of very low-porosity nylon, open at the front end and closed at the back, and cross-sewn with fabric ribs, which form "cells." Most chutes have five, seven, or nine of these double cells, which run either chordwise or spanwise.

The cells, when ram-air inflated, create a pressurized, semirigid wing with upper and lower surfaces and an airfoil section. The wind blows into the open end and pumps the chute up like a balloon. Conceived by Domina Jalbert (in 1964) and developed by Steve Snyder, who was then with the Para-Flite parachute company, this design has steadily taken over the market and is today the most common sports-chute seen—and with good reason. The improvements in maneuverability and safety over the classic round parachute are vast. The ram-air chute is much more reliable at opening, and landings can be made with great finesse; forward speeds of 30 mph can be quickly reduced to zero for a gentle landing. (Round chutes, on the other hand, are much less maneuverable, and have forward speeds of only 5 to 10 mph.) However, a ram-air chute must also be "flown," much more so than its predecessor. A jumper raises and lowers toggles to brake the chute and to turn left or right.

Another improvement in modern chutes is the use of a "slider" that slows down the chute opening. Before the advent of this device, a jumper could suffer an excruciating (and sometimes fatal) shock from the rapid deceleration of his body from 120 mph to less that 10 mph. (No doubt this is why the military calls a parachute an aerodynamic personnel decelerator.) The slider is a rectangular piece of cloth attached to each of the four groups of lines on the canopy by rings (grommets). At the moment of deployment it rests immediately below the canopy, keeping the four lines close together. As the canopy fills, the forces exerted on the lines gradually force the slider down toward the jumper. Because the jumper's speed is decreasing as the chute opens, the opening jolt is considerably lessened by the time the chute is totally filled, although it is impossible to entirely eliminate this sensation **(see Figure 14–5)**.

Canopies are made of nylon, as thin as the finest lingerie. This lightweight material weighs only 1.1 ounces per square yard, but unlike lingerie, which has a breaking strength of about 2 to 10 pounds per square inch (psi), canopy nylon is tough—it takes about 42 psi to pull it apart. A sky diver can choose from a rainbow of colors, blended with various weaves and patterns. Parachute designers are now experimenting with new materials, such as Dacron and Kevlar, favored by sailmakers.

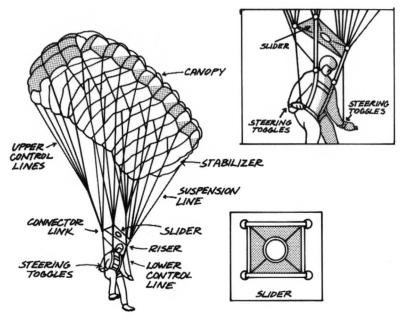

14-5 *How the Ram-Air Chute Works. The slider, a rectangular piece of cloth attached to each of the four groups of lines on the canopy by rings, or grommets, helps slow down the chute opening. Toggles aid in braking and steering the chute.*

Besides the main parachute, all sky divers wear a reserve chute. Unlike the main, which is packed by the parachutist, the reserve must be inspected and packed by a licensed parachute rigger. Students are taught early in their training programs that if any problem occurs with the main chute, they are to "cut it away," and deploy the reserve. (Actually, modern equipment allows a jumper to jettison the main by pulling a canopy release, so a knife is no longer required.)

The Landing

When a parachute landing is done correctly, a jumper converts pain-inducting vertical energy into painless rotational energy. Various techniques are taught that distribute the force of impact evenly throughout the body and so avoid stressing particularly vulnerable parts such as the ankles, knees, and back.

One of the biggest improvements resulting from ram-air technology is the ability of jumpers to "flare" their chutes to slow down for a landing. By pushing the steering toggles down, a jumper reduces both vertical and horizontal speed. These toggles are sometimes made of a hard material, such as wood, and sometimes are large fabric loops. With this type of chute the jumper faces into the wind when landing to reduce ground speed, unlike a round chute, where the jumper lands in the direction of the wind.

Sky divers learn all of these facts and many more as they pursue their first license, a USPA license. For this they must accumulate at least twenty jumps, including a certain amount of free-fall time. They also learn how to pack a parachute, what to do when an unexpected water landing occurs, and other emergency responses. The final step is a written examination.

Dedicated divers then have three other licenses they can pursue: a USPA B license (50 free-fall jumps), USPA C license (100 jumps), and USPA D license (200 jumps). One thousand jumps qualifies a sky diver for a Gold Expert Parachutist Badge, 10,000 for Gold Wings with diamonds, and 20,000 for Gold Wings with rubies. In the United States, only about 3,000 people have the first badge, 800 the second, and 100 the third, so gaining any of these is quite an accomplishment.

Chapter 15
Surfing

Finding the Perfect Wave

"For the true believer, the perfect wave becomes a Holy Grail."
—Ruby Fause, From Driftwood II

Waves lapping at shorelines inspire vacationers to visit ocean
beaches in droves each year. The thousands of miles of empty ocean
soothe our souls; harmonious surf sounds, caused by the collapse of
millions of air bubbles, transport us into peaceful meditation.

Those that live near the water's edge, however, want more than
soothing meditation: they want to harness the sometimes ferocious
energy lying within these rolling tubes of water. A 40-foot wave while
breaking exerts a force of more than two tons per square foot, which, if
converted to power, could fuel the electrical needs of a small city.

Although surfing is believed to have originated with the
Polynesians (who used canoes rather than boards to ride the waves),
surfers in America can thank Hawaiian George Freeth for bringing the
sport to our shores. Described by Jack London as "a young god bronzed
with sunburn," Freeth was enticed here in 1907 by California developer
Henry Huntington, who wanted him to perform in a series of exhibi-
tions promoting the recently constructed Redondo-Los Angeles railroad line. Freeth was so entertaining that not only were the trains filled,
but Californians' addiction to the bohemian lifestyle associated with
surfing was born—and life hasn't been the same since.

All waves form as a result of winds, earthquakes (or underwater
volcanoes), or tidal action. Surfing waves are almost always the result of
wind action, although according to Richard Grigg, an oceanographer
with the University of Hawaii, only about a third of the surfers riding
them know this fact. (Most of the others believe the waves to be caused
by earthquakes.)

When a surfer rides a board across a wave, he or she taps into energy that has built up over thousands of miles of water. As the wind blows across the sea, small ripples form, called cat's paws. These capillary waves create more surface area for the wind to catch, and the ripples grow to become small, steep waves. Then, if wind conditions persist, these waves grow into giant ocean rollers. Winds blowing above 70 knots actually smash the tops off the waves; above 100 knots the waves are torn apart.

Although waves appear to rush forward at great speeds, the water molecules themselves barely move forward. Only the energy form advances rapidly. Like the undulating waves caused in a wheat field by a gentle breeze, or a rope snapped sharply at one end, the molecules only move up and down, while the energy wave moves forward.

In the ocean, as these ripples and waves advance, they combine with other waves of varying sizes. If the waves meet crest-to-crest, they augment one another and grow larger. If they meet crest-to-trough, a cancellation occurs.

The velocity of a wave depends on its wavelength and period. Wavelength is the distance between crests, and period is the time it takes one wave, measured from crest to crest, to pass by a certain point. The speed of advance of any wave equals 1.35 times the square root of the wave's length, where the wave's length is in feet and the speed is in knots. (To convert knots to mph, multiply by 1.15.) In a storm area, and in deep water, typical periods are about 10 seconds. As waves move away from their origination point, and travel from 1,000 to 2,000 miles, the typical period increases up to 20 seconds. As the period increases, so does the wavelength, and the waves may ultimately travel faster than the winds that generated them.

Fetch is the distance a wave travels after its creation and before it breaks on a shore. For a large swell to develop, the fetch normally must be at least 600 to 800 miles. The resulting height of a wave depends largely on the strength of the wind, on the length of time it has blown, and on the fetch.

Although the individual water molecules don't move forward, they are set into a localized, vertical circular motion as the energy of the wave passes over them. The wave form affects these molecules to a depth of one-half the wave's length, and it is only this top layer of water that transmits the energy of the wave. If the water is deeper than one-half the wave's length, the waves are unaffected by the depth of water.

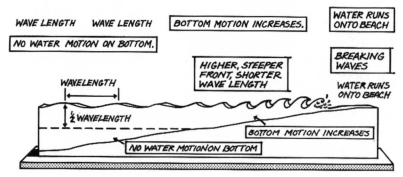

15-1 *Changes That Occur When a Wave Moves Onshore. As a wave approaches shore, the bottom of the swell is slowed down by drag, crests begin to peak, and the wave becomes steeper. When the wave is too steep to support itself, its crest tumbles forward— this is surf.*

A wave's dynamics change radically when it approaches a shore-line, however. The wave slows down, expending energy in moving sand or small grains or rock back and forth along the bottom. The height of the wave also increases and the wavelength decreases. Because the bottom of the swell is slowed down by drag, the crests begin to peak and the wave becomes steeper. When it gets so steep that the wave can no longer support itself, the crest tumbles into the trough. Voila—we have surf **(see Figure 15–1).**

Because strong surfing waves result from storms, a methodical surfer charts storm centers to find the perfect wave. For example, on the northwest shoreline of Hawaii's Oahu (which has a reputation for some of the finest surfing in the world), wintertime storms off Alaska's Aleutian Islands often provide 25- to 30-foot waves. Waimea Bay, a small cove along this shoreline, furnishes particularly lively action because the beach drops off into a two-mile-deep abyss.

In the United States, waves hitting the California shoreline often have traveled from as far away as New Zealand and the South Pacific. Fetch of this length assures smooth rollers for the surfer. East coast waves, on the other hand, tend to be choppier, because of a shorter fetch; Atlantic storms happen closer to shore and the swells don't have time to "smooth out."

Wherever in the world a surfer paddles his board, when the right wave comes along he or she must know how to take off, ride the wave, and pull out.

The Takeoff

Selecting the right wave and taking off from the appropriate spot require a keen sense of timing and a masterful sense of balance on the board. Although many nonsurfers believe that a wave pushes the surfboard along, this isn't true—the surfer actually slides down a hill of water. This hill is not moving toward shore, but up and down.

The size of the wave determines the takeoff point. On a small wave, as long as the surfer is positioned anywhere on the top, he merely has to transfer weight to the front of the board to facilitate a sliding action downhill. On a large wave, however, this doesn't work. The board must be in front of the swell for sliding to occur **(see Figure 15-2)**.

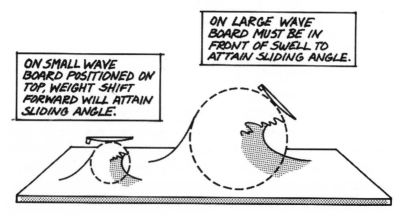

15-2 *How the Size of a Wave Affects a Takeoff. The size of a wave determines a surfer's takeoff point. On a small wave, if the surfer is anywhere on top, he merely has to transfer weight to the front of the board to facilitate a sliding action downhill. On a large wave, the board must be in front of the swell for sliding to occur.*

When the wave arrives, the surfer, who has until now been straddling the board, hops to an upright position. The surfer then shifts his weight forward to facilitate the sliding action.

The Ride

Immediately after taking off, a surfer must turn the board so that he can skim across the face of the wave. It is during this turn that purling most often happens, which is when the nose of the board goes below the surface of the water, causing the board to flip.

To turn, the surfer changes his stance and the position of his feet. Four balance points come into play. The balls and heels of both feet are used to maneuver the board. Pressure is put on one side of the board, causing drag, which in turn forces a turn. Changing the position of the arms can also affect the weight distribution. After turning, a board is "trimmed out" so that it lies more or less flat on the water's surface.

Most rides last about 15 seconds, with the surfer traveling 25 to 35 mph. Exceptions abound, though, and at Matanchen Bay near San Blas, in Mexico, conditions arise about five times a year that allow rides exceeding two minutes, with the surfer cruising approximately 5,700 feet.

The Pullout

A proper pullout is essential, if for no other reason than to keep the surfer from losing his board. This is important to other surfers, too, because loose, flying surfboards are one of the biggest hazards of the sport. Depending on where on the wave the rider is, the wave may wall up and start to crash in front of him. He must then be prepared to pull out and get beyond the crashing surf. (Wipeout occurs when a wave breaks on top of a surfer, or otherwise knocks him off the board.)

Many different techniques are used for pulling out, all with the ultimate goal of turning the surfer back up the face of the wave and over the crest.

A surfer modifies these three steps depending on the nature of the surf. Although big waves can be intimidating, size alone doesn't determine how difficult a wave is to ride. A small surf can be challenging because there is little time after the takeoff to effect a turn before hitting the trough. Whether a wave is considered monstrous also depends on the beach under discussion. An 8-foot wave at Laguna Beach, California, is huge; a 10-foot at San Onofre, some 20 miles farther south, is routine. Large waves do, however, require an adaptation of special techniques, such as riding close to the top of the wave so that pulling out is possible.

A special type of wave, called a tsunami, fascinates both surfers and nonsurfers. Tsunamis are actually seismic sea waves, although they are often erroneously called tidal waves. (Tsunami is a Japanese word; tsu means overflowing, and nami means wave.) Actually, their motion (and the consequent damage they inflict) have nothing to do with tidal actions. Rather, they are generated by underwater earthquakes. Barely perceptible as they speed across the surface of the water, often at speeds of 400 to 450 mph, these waves carry along awsome stores of energy, and more than 150 miles can separate two successive crests. At the shoreline, the water typically recedes for a few minutes (the seismic trough reaching land), and then an enormous wave strikes—up to 200 feet high, but normally tens of feet high. The largest on record was about 278 feet high, occurring in 1771 off Ishigaki Island. An 850-ton block of coral was thrown 1.3 miles.

Regardless of where they occur, big waves are impressive. One of the largest on record happened in February, 1933, when a U.S. Navy tanker, the U.S.S. *Ramapo*, was traveling to San Diego from Manila. The ship's log recorded steady winds of 30 to 50 knots, and a falling barometer. Huge seas subsequently developed, but the tanker, being 478 feet long, took them in stride. Then one of the lookouts on the bridge saw an enormous wave overtaking them from astern. The ensuing slant of the ship, as the wave passed under it, put the lookout level with the ship's crows nest. Simple geometry later showed that the wave was at least 112 feet high, with a speed of about 55 knots. The maximum wave height a surfer can ride is about 35 feet, so this was not your perfect surfing wave.

Sharks and Surfers

Attacks by sharks on surfers are rare, but not unknown. Marine biologist John McCosker, an ex-surfer, says one reason may be that from below a surfer looks just like a shark's favorite food: a seal. Surfboards, which formerly were a long nine feet, now measure only five to six feet, and sport multiple fins and split tails. When a surfer is straddling the board and paddling, it is easy to see how the silhouette from below could look like a seal. This mistaken identity is particularly likely because, although they can see extremely well, sharks are farsighted and anything close is usually out of focus.

Research has shown that safety colors, such as international orange, attract sharks. In fact, researchers call this color "yum-yum yellow." Sharks are also attracted to buckles, CO_2 cartridges, and other shiny objects. Metal objects generate small electric fields in salt water, particularly if they are attached to a battery. Some researchers believe this field compels a shark to bite.

Sharks possess the most sensitive electroreceptors ever discovered in the entire animal kingdom. So acute is this ability that they can sense an electric field equivalent to that of a flashlight battery connected to electrodes spaced a thousand miles apart in the ocean. Since the act of breathing (through either gills or lungs) produces a small but measurable amount of bioelectricity, this extraordinary sense has allowed sharks to become one of the most skilled predators alive.

Surfers should note that there is some indication that sharks may be more likely to strike in areas where the water is unusually warm or where the fish supply is down.

Various shark repellents have been developed through the years, most of which have only a limited effect. Some stun guns proved to be more dangerous to the diver than to the shark, when they showed a tendency to discharge accidentally. Recent developments look more promising, however, and include a hand-held stun gun invented by Lyle Mendocino. This "gun" injects a pulsating current under the skin of the shark, which reportedly makes it quickly leave the area. More beneficial to a surfer is the discovery of a detergent-like material that seriously deters a shark's inclination to attack. The chemical may ultimately be made available in the form of a slow-releasing deodorant.

While much hullabaloo is made about shark attacks, normally fewer than twenty-five people are killed by them each year. On the other hand, commercial shark catches in the United States increased dramatically in the 1980s and 1990s. Chances are much greater that you'll be having shark for dinner tonight than vice versa.

Chapter 16
Tennis

What a Racket

"The problem with standardized instruction is that it confuses students who see the pros do things differently from the way instructors advise. The fact is that I almost never hit the ball exactly the same way twice."

—*Bjorn Borg*

After hollering at the lineman for calling a serve out, John McEnroe positioned himself for his second serve. As he tossed the ball into the air, reaching his arm back for the swing, power radiated from his perfect athletic form. The rising racket sped toward the ball at 325 mph. Suddenly, accompanied by the famous McEnroe grunt, ball and racket collided, and the ball sizzled toward the net at a brutal 150 mph.

As it crossed the net, air resistance slowed the ball to 100 mph. Still, it had enough velocity to thunder into the opponent's court, bounce off the line, and leave the area at 45 mph, unscathed by the opponent's racket. An ace for John McEnroe.

Actually, it rarely happens like this. First, a study by Dennis Lendrem, an animal behaviorist at the University of Nottingham, shows that McEnroe's silent serves are almost twice as successful as his grunt serves. Hence, if he grunts, he is less likely to make an ace. Second, a study done by Richard Cox, a psychologist at Kansas State University, shows that an intimidated or abused lineman is more likely to make mistakes in his calls. Because the second serve fell on the line, quite possibly the lineman would have faced further abuse by McEnroe for calling this one out, too.

It appears that McEnroe's noises, whether serving grunts or tempestuous tirades, did little to improve his game. He may not have had great control over his mouth—though admittedly he got better with age—he nevertheless clearly had great control over four other major elements that affect a tennis game: the racket, the grip, the spin put on the ball, and strategy.

The Racket

In the last five to ten years, major ski makers have taken to manufacturing tennis rackets. In large part this is because the equipment for both sports has similar design constraints. Both have a propensity for vibration, which adversely affects the quality of play, and both benefit from light, strong materials.

Howard Head, famous for revolutionizing the skiing industry with his metal sandwich skis, also revolutionized the game of tennis when he invented the aluminum racket in 1972. Head's goal was to design a racket that diminished the tendency of a racket to twist in the hands when hit off center (torque). Actually, after selling his ski company in 1970, his immediate goal was to retire and live a leisurely life playing tennis and enjoying other fun activities. But fortunately for tennis players, his retirement was short-lived when Head became frustrated with the way his racket behaved, and he hauled out his drawing board to solve the problem. After grappling with the problem of torque both in the daylight hours and in his dreams, he found a solution: a larger racket would move mass away from the center of the racket and make it "more forgiving" and less subject to torque, both by reducing the angular acceleration and increasing the rotational inertia.

The problem with this racket, which was two inches wider, three inches longer, and had 20 percent more string area than conventional rackets, was that it cracked easily. Adding wood didn't help—the racket just became too heavy. So Head turned to extruded aluminum alloy for the frame. He patented his racket in 1976 and granted the Prince Manufacturing Company production rights. The new Prince racket took the market by storm **(see Figure 16–1)**.

Despite Head's improvement, and others made subsequently, the perfect racket hasn't yet been designed. The problem is in locating the racket's sweet spot. Although a player senses where this spot is by noticing where the strokes feel best, scientists aren't content with this defini-

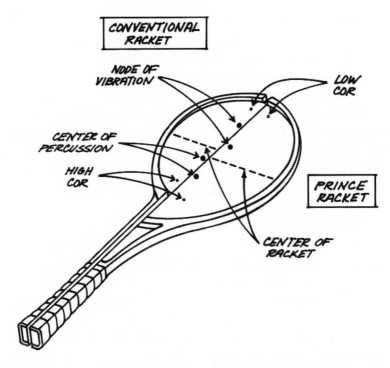

CONVENTIONAL
RACKET

NODE OF
VIBRATION

LOW
COR

CENTER OF
PERCUSSION

HIGH
COR

PRINCE
RACKET

CENTER OF
RACKET

16-1 *Prince Versus Conventional Racket. An ideal racket would have all three sweet spots located in its center, with the power region and nodal region covering most of the face. A Prince racket comes closer to this ideal than the conventional racket.*

tion. They want to know precisely where on the racket the ball should hit for maximum results, and why maximum power is thereby obtained.

An especially curious physicist is Howard Brody, of the University of Pennsylvania. He has extensively studied tennis rackets and says there are three sweet spots. One is located where the racket produces the maximum rebound power, or where the coefficient of restitution (COR) is highest. (See Chapter 1: Baseball, for more information on CORs.) Brody calls this area the power region. A player can easily obtain this measurement by dropping a ball onto the face of a racket and measuring the rebound height. The COR is calculated by taking the square root of the rebound height divided by the drop height. The higher the COR, the greater the rebound power.

The second sweet spot is at the racket's center of percussion (COP). Players are most sensitive to this spot, because a hit here transmits the least shock. Missing it causes the hand to feel jarring vibrations. Brody says this is because if the ball hits between the COP and throat of the racket, the handle is pushed back toward the player's hand; if the ball hits between the top and the COP, the handle moves toward the net. If the hit occurs at the COP (or, actually, between a pair of conjugate points), the forces balance. Not only does such a stroke feel good to the player, but it also maximizes the amount of momentum transferred to the ball. According to Brody, this area is about two inches toward the handle from the center of the racket.

The third sweet spot is at the racket's vibrational dead zone, the so-called nodes of vibration. When this spot is hit, high-frequency vibrations between 125 and 170 hertz (Hz), depending on the brand of racket, are minimized because the waves cancel each other out. (Vibrations of a higher frequency are absorbed so quickly that they are not a problem.) If the ball makes contact outside this dead zone, vibrations travel up and down the racket, sometimes causing a loss of control. Player fatigue can also result. Players can find this on their own rackets by dropping a ball from a height of 8 inches onto the racket face, held parallel to the ground and face up. The area generating the least amount of vibration should be obvious. For most rackets, the nodes' location is about 5.2 inches from the racket tip, or about 4 to 5 inches from the COP, toward the center of the racket.

Brody says an ideal racket would have all three sweet spots located in its center, with the power region and nodal region covering most of the face of the racket.

One reason the Prince racket so inspired players is that it inadvertently had a much larger sweet spot (based on the COR) than its predecessors. The center of percussion was also larger, which in effect moved it toward the center of the racket.

Loosening string tension can increase a racket's COR, but only up to a point. Jack Groppel, of the University of Illinois, along with various associates, recently tested twelve rackets and found that the highest COR corresponded to a string tension of 40 pounds. (Bjorn Borg reportedly uses 80 pounds, not to increase the velocity on the ball, but because he feels it gives him extra control.) Various studies have placed the ideal tension from a low of 40 pounds to a high of 55 pounds.

One problem with oversize rackets is the elusiveness of a perfect string design. Although thinner strings perform better, they also wear out quickly. Most tennis players prefer natural gut strings, but these are costly and wear out especially rapidly. Hence, most recreational players content themselves with synthetic strings. Manufacturers process "gut," or natural strings, from the intestines of sheep, cows or pigs. It takes about 33 feet of finished product to string a racket. Both 15- and 16-gauge strengths are available, the latter being heavier and more frequently used by recreational players. Modern synthetic strings are made of a variety of components and may have a solid core, a composite string core, or an oil-filled core.

Since Head's origination of the Prince racket, other manufacturers have modernized their designs and players now have a wide variety of styles, prices, and high-tech features to choose from. Not only are mid-sized (85 to 95 square inches) and oversized (106 to 115 square inches) rackets the norm, but materials range from graphite to ceramics, Kevlar, and Twaron—all developed with an intent to either increase power or decrease shock to a player's hand and arm. Frame thickness has doubled to a wide 1.75 inches on some rackets.

Many players choose the lightest racket available, but this may be a mistake. A lighter racket transfers more vibration to a player's arm, increasing the likelihood of developing tennis elbow. The heavier the racket, the more it absorbs these damaging vibrations. Rackets are now so sophisticated that one brand features a liquid-filled frame, and when the head is up, the liquid flows to the throat, making the head lighter (useful in moving the racket faster for high volleys and overheads). On a ground stroke or low volley, the liquid moves to the head, adding weight and stability to that area.

Although today graphite is the dominant material used in wide-body rackets (making them two or three times stiffer than wood rackets), players experiencing stress on their elbows and shoulders may find relief by switching to a racket that includes fiberglass in its composition,

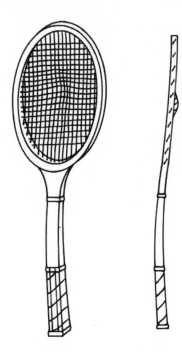

16-2 *How a Racket Deforms (Exaggerated Scale). When a ball hits the racket's face, both the strings and the racket are significantly deformed. The ball flattens almost completely against the strings, which act like a trampoline; string tension increases and the racket deforms.*

because this material absorbs shock better. Looser strings may also help.

Some players customize their rackets by placing lead tape in strategic spots to vary the weight and balance, which in turn can increase the size and direction of the sweet spot. (The sweet spot moves in the direction of the weights.) If a player favors the baseline, for example, having a racket that is top-heavy can be beneficial; a net player may want the increased maneuverability that comes with a lighter head. A player interested in adding stability for off-center shots may choose to place three-inch strips of tape at the 3 o'clock and 9 o'clock positions. MIT professor Ram Ramnath, head of the World Tennis racket lab-test program, cautions that "lead tape is for the more sophisticated player who knows exactly what he wants in a racket."

Regardless of what a racket is made of or how it is customized, when a ball hits the racket's face, significant deformations occur, both to the strings, which act like a trampoline; string tension increases and the racket deforms **(see Figure 16–2).**

The strings then snap back into place, imparting a tremendous amount of elastic energy to the ball—enough to make it leave a pro's racket at 150 mph. The contact interval is 4 to 5 milliseconds (msec). The racket is much slower in returning to its original form (about 15 msec). By this time, the ball is long gone, so this recoil does not contribute energy to the ball. (Groppel has found that the time of contact on an oversized racket is between 5.2 and 8.6 msec, up to twice the interval found in conventional rackets—but still faster than the time it takes the racket to recoil.)

Because a stiffer racket deforms less, it "steals" less of the elastic energy from the strings and thus from the ball. The more tension on the strings, the less deformation occurs to both the strings and racket, because the string tension in effect stiffens the racket. Conversely, lower tension in the strings combined with a stiffer racket increases the COR. (A larger racket must still have higher string tension than a conventional racket, however.) "To get the highest speed into the ball when you hit it," Brody says, "you want the strings to store the energy by deflecting. At a lower tension, the strings will deflect more, the ball will deform less, and the ball will bounce back higher."

Although many tennis racket manufacturers tout the ability of their product to quickly dampen vibrations, Brody says that such damping has a minor effect. "The hand holding the racket damps out the oscillations in about 20 to 30 milliseconds," he says, "which is much faster than the frame material itself, which damps the amplitude of the oscillations to half value in 180 to 750 milliseconds, depending on the racket."

A "perfect" racket won't lead to perfect games. Most experts believe consistent good placement will win more games than speed and power alone. Jimmy Connors, after all, won hundreds of matches using his inexpensive Wilson T-2000 racket, and he continued to use it even after the company quit making them.

The Grip

Which grip is the best? Bjorn Borg says, "I believe tennis is a game of instinct and common sense rather than proper grips and tedious tips."

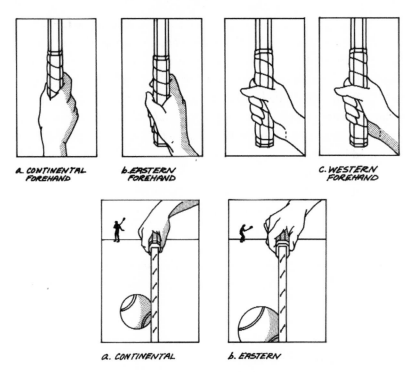

16-3   *Tennis Grips. Continental, Eastern and Western forehand grips are shown from the player's view (top). Continental and Eastern backhand grips from the playing view (bottom).*

Jimmy Connors agrees. "After all my years in the game, I don't know what kind of grip I use to hit the ball."

In fact, Connors used a variation of the Continental grip for all of his strokes; Borg used the Western grip for his forehand, Eastern for his backhand, and Continental for his volleys, serve, and overhead. Both used a two-handed backhand.

The point they are making is that players should use a grip they find most comfortable, and not worry if it is a "regular" form. If a player has a strong urge to classify the grip, though, the following are general guidelines:

The Continental grip originated on European clay courts and is popular with grass-court players. The grip is the same for forehand and backhand shots; hence, it is useful when there is little time between shots to change grips. Because this grip requires strong wrists and excellent timing, players known for consistent control and placement favor it, more so than those known for their powerful ground strokes. (Connors is an exception here.)

The Western grip originated on the cement courts of California and is well suited to the high-bouncing balls this hard surface produces. Some players use the grip for both forehand and backhand shots, but because the grip puts extreme tension on the elbow, use of it on backhand strokes may contribute to tennis elbow.

The eastern grip originated on courts in the eastern United States. Known as the "shake hands" grip, it is the most popular grip taught by tennis professionals. Of the three grips, it is the most versatile on all surfaces, and most adaptable to individual playing styles. To change from a forehand to a backhand grip, the racket is turned a quarter turn counterclockwise (clockwise for a lefthander) and the thumb is extended to serve as a brace along the handle **(see Figure 16–3)**.

Spin

Spin is a desired element in tennis because it can give a player more control over the ball and because it increases the unpredictability of the ball's motion after the bounce. To that end, players attempt to generate and control backspin (underspin), topsin (overspin) and sidespin (slice). Each hit has only so much energy, however, and the more that is put into ball rotation, the less is available for forward speed and drive.

A ball flying through the air is subject to air pressure differences that generate lift. Bernoulli's theorem describes this phenomenon, and is discussed elsewhere is the book. If the ball is rotating, it is also subject to the Magnus effect. Gustav Magnus developed this theory in 1852, and it states that the lift created on a rotating ball moving through air will deflect the ball in the direction of the spin. In other words, a ball with a clockwise spin will swerve to the left. In a like manner, backspin causes the ball to rise, and topspin causes the ball to drop (sink) **(see Figure 16–4)**.

A player puts topspin on the ball by "brushing" upward on the back of the ball with the racket at impact held vertical to the ground. Such a

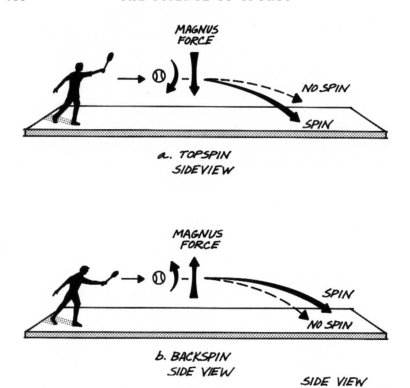

16-4 *Magnus Force on Topspin and Backspin. Because of Magnus force, the lift creat-ed on a rotating ball moving through the air deflects the ball in the direction of the spin. A ball spinning clockwise will swerve to the right and one spinning counterclockwise will swerve to the left. Similarly, backspin causes the ball to rise and topspin makes it sink.*

ball will drop, much in the manner a curveball in baseball "breaks." When the tennis ball bounces on the other side of the court, one of two reactions occur: If the linear speed is greater than the rotational speed, the ball will continue forward after it bounces, but at a slower speed than it would have without spin, because the rotational speed subtracts from the linear speed. (With pure topspin, the rotational velocity is in an opposite direction from the linear velocity.) But if the ball's rotational velocity is greater than its linear velocity, on contact the ball will accel-erate and gain speed. In both cases, the ball bounces higher than it would have without spin.

Backspin (underspin) is generated by moving the racket from high to low; that is, brushing downward on the back of the ball. The more "open" the racket face and the more pronounced the downward swing plane, the more backspin will be put on the ball. Backspin makes the ball rise in flight. When the ball lands, the forward linear motion and the rotating motion are in the same direction and upon contact combine, but because the additional speed also increases the frictional forces, the ball leaves the ground at a slower velocity than it would have without spin. It also rebounds at a lower trajectory. If the rotational velocity is high enough, the ball may even reverse direction when it bounces.

A player generates pure sidespin, or slice, by brushing the ball from left to right (or from right to left) and high to low. The ball swerves in the direction of its rotation. The racket moves from high to low, just before and after contact, though almost imperceptibly. The effect of sidespin is most evident when the ball bounces, but the sideways curving motion down the court can be seen on shots with maximum spin.

Some players try to "roll" the ball with their racket to induce spin. This is of itself ineffective because the time of contact between the racket and ball is too short for this action to have any significant effect. The only way to generate significant spin is to have the racket's vertical plane move up or down, or for slices, sideways. However, many players combine the two actions to great advantage.

Strategy

Winning a tennis match involves more than just powering the ball forward, although power certainly doesn't hurt. Strategy is important, too, in such areas as unearthing the opponent's weak spots and playing to them. Patience pays off in this game.

Bill Tym, while president of the U.S. Professional Tennis Association, found that 80 percent of all shots by pros land within the dotted lines shown in **Figure 16–5**. Pros don't aim for the remaining 20-percent zone, their hits just land in that area 20 percent of the time. Bjorn Borg says, "If I strike a ball that lands a foot from my opponent's base, it's an accident, because I'm only aiming for two yards past the

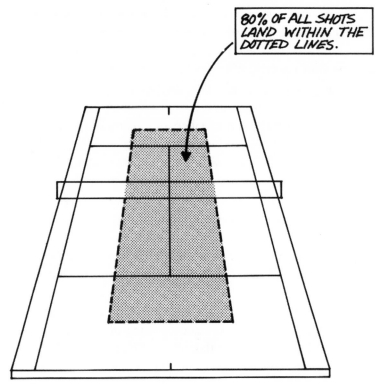

16-5 *Most Used Area of Court. Eighty percent of all shots land within the dotted lines.*

service box—for security." Tym recommends that players strive for consistency and success by establishing an aim point well inside the baseline, but not so short that it allows one's opponent to come in and attack the net. An optimal placement for most players is two to three feet inside the baseline.

Tym also believes that the first consideration in choosing a shot should be whether a player can make the shot, and the second should be where on the court the opponent is. He believes many players reverse these elements, to the detriment of their games.

Of course, players should always try to win points whenever they play. Some points are more important than others, though, and an important part of any strategy to perform best when attempting to make these critical points.

Critical points are the first and fourth points of each game, and especially the game point. Critical games are the first game, the seventh game, and the game for set. The scoring system is such that a player winning the most points can still actually lose the match. If, for example, on the games player A wins, his opponent (player B) scores no points—a love game—and on the games player B wins, A takes him to deuce each time, the player A may lose even though he has won the most points. Likewise, a player can win more games than his opponent and still lose the match. A score of 7-5, 0-6, and 7-5, for example, represents 14 games won by the victor and 16 by the loser.

The Surface: Hard Versus Soft

Tennis is unique in international sports because the surface played on varies depending where in the world the tournament is held.

Three different "speeds" of court surfaces—fast, medium, and slow—almost make the game three separate sports.

Grass courts are "fast." Today, of the major tournaments, only the Australian Open and Wimbledon are played on grass courts. (Less than 1 percent of the courts in the United States are grass, though at one time the U.S. Open was played on this surface.)

Balls bounce fast and erratically on grass, and rebound with low trajectories. The ball also skids a bit each time it lands, unless it hits a bald spot, where it "grips," which is part of the erratic nature of the surface. Players avoid topspin, because it makes the ball bounce higher (but is slowed down too much to be effective unless really clobbered) and puts it more easily in the opponent's reach. Players say to "pull out your power serve and reach the net first" when playing on grass. The surface encourages savage serve-and-volley games, and rallies are generally short-lived. After the first week of play at Wimbledon, however, the grass wears down so much that the surface plays almost like clay.

Clay is a "slow" surface. Outside the United States, 70 percent of the tennis courts in the world are clay, including those at the French Open. Americans accustomed to the hard courts here seldom win this tournament. Games played on clay seem to move more slowly and, because the ball bounces higher, players have plenty of time to get into position. Baseline rallies sometimes seem endless, so patience and stamina are essential. Strategy is more important here than power.

The ball slides on the grass at Wimbledon, but on clay courts at the French Open it is the player who slides. A player must watch his traction as well as the ball. An ability to hit good ground strokes with topspin pays off here because clay does not lend itself to the serve-and-volley games as well as faster surfaces. Two pluses for clay courts are that they reduce wear and tear on the body, and on hot days heat is absorbed, rather than being reflected into players' faces.

Hard courts, such as those played on at the U.S. Open, are medium-speed courts. Balls bounce true and a player's traction is true. Most of the courts in the United States are of two varieties: composition, which is an asphalt base with an acrylic coat, or cement, usually also topped with an acrylic or polyurethane coat. Acrylic coatings depend on a mixture of sand and water to give the court texture. This coating also makes the ball bounce more slowly than it would in a parking lot.

Hard courts definitely place more strain on a player's body. Martina Navratilova said she practiced less for U.S. Open tournaments because "hard courts can kill you."

She also has this advice for players confronted with an unfamiliar surface. "Keep your game simple. Shorten your strokes. As you get comfortable with the court, lengthen your strokes." She adds that unless you are playing on clay or slow cement, it is almost always better to keep strokes short and low.

Pros often adjust the string tension on their rackets for different court surfaces. Generally, strings are looser for slow surfaces (clay) and tighter for faster surfaces (cement and grass).

Good clay players seem to have an easier time adjusting to other surfaces than do hard-court players. Because clay courts are so prevalent outside the United States, American players may lose their edge in international tournaments as the Association of Tennis Professionals starts to shift more games to European locales.

Bibliography

General References

Brancazio, P.J., *Sports Science*. New York: Simon & Schuster, 1984

Schrier, E., and W. F. Allman (eds.) *Newton at the Bat*. New York: Charles Scribner's Sons, 1984.

Torrey, L., *Stretching the Limits*, New York: Dodd, Mead & Co. 1985.

Young, M. (ed.), *Guinness Book of Sports Records, 1991*. Guinness Publishing Co., (New York: Facts-on-File)

Chapter 1: Baseball

Adler, B., *Baseball Wit*. New York: Crown Publishers, 1986

Allman, W.F., "Pitching Rainbows." In *Newton at the Bat*, E. Schrier and W. F. Allman (eds.), New York: Charles Scribner's Sons, 1984.

Allman, W. F., "What Makes a Knuckleball Dance?" *Newton at the Bat*, E. Schrier and W. F. Allman (eds.), New York: Charles Scribner's Sons, 1984.

Binette, W., *"Knuckler": The Phil Niekro Story*. Atlanta, Georgia: Hallux Publishing, 1970.

Hall, S. S., "Baseball's Dirty Tricks." *Newton at the Bat*, E. Schrier and W. F. Allman (eds.), New York: Charles Scribner's Sons, 1984.

Kindel, S. (ed.), "The Hardest Single Act in All of Sports." *Forbes* 132 (Sept. 26, 1983).

Kluger, J., "What's Behind the Home Run Boom?" *Discover 9* (April 1988).

"Knuckleballs." *Scientific American 257* (July 1987).

Niekro, P., and T. Bird, *Knuckleballs*. New York: Freundlich Books, 1986.

Rue, W. *Weather of the Pacific Coast*. Mercer Island, Washington: The Writing Works, 1978.

Seaver, T., and L. Lowenfish, *The Art of Pitching*. New York: Hearst Books, 1984.

Sloan, D. (ed.), *Official Baseball Guide 1988*. St. Louis, Missouri: The Sporting News, 1988.

Thorn, J., and B. Carroll (eds.) *The Whole Baseball Catalogue*. New York: Simon & Schuster, 1990.

Thorn, J., and J. Holway, *The Pitcher*. New York: Prentice-Hall, 1987.

Torrey, L., *Stretching the Limits.* New York: Dodd, Mead & Co., 1985.

Waggoner, G., K. Moloney, and H. Howard, *Baseball by the Rules.* Dallas: Taylor Publishing Co., 1987.

Will, G., *Men at Work.* Macmillan, 1990.

Chapter 2: Basketball

Abdul-Jabbar, K., *Kareem Abdul-Jabbar,* New York: Random House, 1990.

Barzman, S., *505 Basketball Questions.* New York: Walker & Co., 1981.

Brancazio, P.J., "Physics of Basketball." *American Journal of Physics 49* (1981).

Johnson, E. J., Jr., *Magic Touch.* New York: Addison-Wesley 1989.

Kertes, T., "Basketball '80s (The Glorious Decade)." *Sports 80* (Oct. 1989).

Michener, J., *Sports in America.* New York: Random House, 1976.

Russel, B., and T. Branch, *Second Wind.* New York: Random House, 1979.

Suinn, R. M., "Behavior Rehersal Training for Ski Racers." *Behavior Therapy 3* (1972).

Suinn, R. M., "Removing Emotional Obstacles to Learning and Performance by Visuo-motor Behavior Rehearsal." *Behavior Therapy 3* (1972).

Torrey, L., *Stretching the Limits.* New York: Dodd, Mead & Co., 1985.

Chapter 3: Bicycling

Abt, S., *LeMond: The Incredible Comeback of an American Hero.* New York: Random House, 1990.

Anderson, O., "A Question That's Gone Round & Round," *Women's Sports & Fitness 11* (Jan./Feb. 1989).

DeLong, F., *DeLong's Guide to Bicycles and Bicycling.* Radnor, Pennsylvania: Chilton Book Co., 1978.

Drake, G., "Aero Answers." *Bicycling 31* (May 1990).

Johnson, S., "Cadence." *Bicycling 30* (April 1989).

Kukoda, J., "Better Braking." *Bicycling 30* (Sept. 1989).

Kyle, C. R., "How Friction Slows a Bike." *Bicycling 29* (June 1988).

Kyle, C.R., "How Weight Affects Bicycle Speed." *Bicycling* (May 1988).

Kyle, C. R., "The Limits of Leg Power." *Bicycling* (Oct. 1990).

Langford, J. S., "Daedalus: The Making of a Legend." *Technology Review 91* (Oct. 1988).

LeMond, G., and K. Gordis, *Greg LeMond's Complete Book of Bicycling*. New York: G. P. Putnam's Sons, 1987.

McGurn, J., *On Your Bicycle*. New York: Facts-on-File Publications, 1987.

Perlman, E., "Building Better Bikes." In *Newton at the Bat*, E. Schrier and W. F. Allman (eds.), New York: Charles Scribner's Sons, 1984.

Chapter 4: Billiards

Allman, W. F., "Pool Hall Physics." *Science 84.* 5 (March 1984).

Freedman, L. (ed.), "Straight Pool: Rack'em Up." In *Best Sports Stories 1988*, St. Louis: The Sporting News, 1988.

Mizerak, S., *Steve Mizerak's Pocket Billiards Tips and Trick Shots*. Chicago: Contemporary Books, 1982.

Neary, J., "The Ex-Hustler Whose Pool Cues Are a Fine Art." *Smithsonian* 20 (Nov. 1989).

Walker, J., "The Physics of the Follow, the Draw, and Masse (in Billiards and Pool)." *Scientific American* 249 (July 1983).

Chapter 5: Boomerang

Bower, B., "Prehistoric Tusk: Early Boomerang?" *Science News* 132 (Oct. 3, 1987).

Hall, S. S., "Boom in 'Rangs Launches Old Toy into New Orbit." *Smithsonian* 15 (June, 1984)

Hess, F., "The Aerodynamics of Boomerangs." *Scientific American* 219 (Nov. 1968).

"High Tech Boomerang (Products to Watch)." *Fortune* 122 (July 2, 1990).

Robson, D., "Many Happy Returns." *Science 83* 4 (March 1983).

Rule, B., and E. Darnell, *Boomerang: How to Throw, Catch, and Make It*. New York: Workman, 1985.

Walker, J., "The Amateur Scientist." *Scientific American* 240 (March/April 1979).

Chapter 6: Darts

Brackin, I. L., and W. Fitzgerald, *All About Darts*. Matteson, IL: Greatlakes Living Press, 1975.

Crow, L. T., and C. Ball, "Alcohol State-Dependency and Automatic Reactivity." *Psychophysiology* 12 (Nov. 1975).

Greene, C., "The Unsocial Drinker: Another Round?" *Psychology Today* 21 (March 1987).

Hull, J. G., "A Self-Awarness Model of the Causes and Effects of Alcohol Consumption." *Journal of Abnormal Psychology* 90 (Dec. 1981).

Jefferson, D. J., "Throwing Darts Without Booze Unquestionably Misses the Point." *The Wall Street Journal,* April 18, 1991.

Pittel, L., "Smart Darts Revisited." *Forbes* 135 (March 11, 1985).

Tierney, J., "The Finer Points of Darts." In *Newton at the Bat,* E. Schrier and W. F. Alman (eds.), New York: Charles Scribner's Sons, 1984.

Wichman, H., and P. Lizotte, "Effects of Mental Practice and Locus of Control on Performance of Dart Throwing." *Perceptual and Motor Skills* 56 (1983).

Chapter 7: Diving the Depths

Brandt, R., "High Fashion Meets High Tech—Underwater." *Business Week,* Sept. 4, 1989.

Davis, J. C., "Decompression Sickness in Sport Scuba Diving." *The Physician and Sportsmedicine* 16 (Feb. 1988).

The New Science of Skin and Scuba Diving, 5th rev. ed. Chicago: Association Press/ Follett Publishing Co., 1980.

Roos, R., "Are the Risks of Sport Scuba Diving Being Underestimated?" *The Physician And Sportsmedicine* 17 (July 1989).

Samson, R. L., and M. B. Strauss, "Decompression Sickness: An Update." *The Physician and Sportsmedicine.* 14 (March 1986).

Springer, R. R., *The Digest Book of Skin & Scuba Diving.* Northfield, IL: DBI Books, 1979.

Chapter 8: Football

Bakke, J., "The Mechanics of the Bomb." *Popular Mechanics.* 165 (Nov. 1988).

Brancazio, P. J., "The Physics of Kicking a Football." *The Physics Teacher* 23 (Oct. 1985).

Cain, T. E., MD, B. Dorzis, and J. Meins, "Use of the Air-Inflated Jacket in Football," *The American Journal of Sports Medicine* (: 4 (1981).

Clerkin, D., *Football Humor*. self-published, New Britain, Connecticut, 1989.

Demak, R., "Run and Chute." *Sports Illustrated* 74 (May 27, 1991).

Duda, M., "Study: More Grid Injuries on Grass." *The Physician and Sportsmedicine* 16 (April 1988).

Eskow, D., "Dressed to Kill." *Popular Mechanics* 160 (Oct. 1983).

Gollnick, P. D., and H. Matoba, "The Muscle Fiber Composition of Skeletal Muscle As a Predictor of Athletic Success." *The American Journal of Sports Medicine* 12: 3 (1984).

Gonyea, W. J., "Role of Exercise in Inducing Increases in Skeletal Muscle Fiber Number." *Journal of Applied Physiology* 48: 3 (1980).

Horn, J. C., "Do Black Shirts Make Bad Guys?" *Psychology Today* 22 (Nov. 1988).

Lidz, F., "Life Is a Ball Here in Ada." *Sports Illustrated* 73 (Sept. 10, 1990).

McCarthy, P., "Artifical Turf: Does It Cause More Injuries?" *The Physician and Sportsmedicine* 17 (Oct. 1989).

Murry, C. J. (ed.), "New Materials Take the Field: Footballs Go Soft." *Design News* 46 (Nov. 19, 1990).

Radford, P., "The Nature and Nurture of a Sprinter." *New Scientist* (Aug. 2, 1984).

Rapoport, R., "Artificial Turf: Is the Grass Greener?" *Newton at the Bat*, E. Schrier and W. F. Allman (eds.), New York: Charles Scribner's Sons, 1984.

Rodeo, S. A., et. Al., "Turf Toe: Diagnosis and Treatment." *The Physician and Sportsmedicine* 17 (April 1989).

Torrey, L., *Stretching the Limits*. New York: Dodd, Mead & Co., 1985.

Underwood, J., "Just an Awful Toll." *Sports Illustrated* 63 (Aug. 12, 1985).

Chapter 9: Frisbee

Bowermaster, J., "They Fly Through the Air with the Greatest of Ease." *Sports Illustrated* 70 (May 8, 1989).

Danna, M., "After 30 High-Flying Years, the Frisbee Still Soars." *Sports Illustrated* 66 (May 11, 1987).

Gold, M., "The Fairy Tale Physics of Frisbees." *Science 82* 3 (June 1982).

Hall, S. M., "You Can Sail Through Willie Williams' Frisbee Course, but Not Without Learning Physics." *People Weekly* 15 (June 15, 1981).

Neff, C. (ed.), "Reinventing the Wheel." *Sports Illustrated* 72 (June 11, 1990).

Schuurmans, M., "Flight of the Frisbee." *New Scientist* 127 (July 1990).

Chapter 10: Gliding

Bowers, P., *Modern Soaring Guide*. Blue Ridge Summit, Pennsylvania: Tab Books, 1979.

Hunter, L., "The Art and Physics of Soaring." *Physics Today* 37 (April 1984).

Piggott, D., *Gliding*. Totowa, New Jersey: Barnes & Noble Books, 1986.

Weiner, E., "On Limber Wings Do Spirits Soar." *Flying* 114 (May 1987).

Chapter 11: Golf

Abrahams, J., "Read 'em or Weep." *Golf* 33 (May 1991).

Aksamit, G., and W. Husak, "Feedback Influences on the Skill of Putting." *Perceptual and Motor Skills* 56 (1983).

Corcoran, M., "The Model Explained." *Golf Illustrated* (Feb. 1988).

Diagram Group, *The Sports Fan's Ultimate Book on Sports Comparisons*. New York: St. Martin's Press, 1982.

Diaz, J., "Perils of Putting." *Sports Illustrated* 70 (April 3, 1989).

Fisman, L., "Physics of Golf." *Science Digest* 94 (June 1986).

Gallwey, W. T., *The Inner Game of Golf*. New York: Random House, 1981.

Holmes, B. W., "Putting: How a Golf Ball and Hole Interact." *American Journal of Physics* 59 (Feb. 1991).

Leacock, S., "Mathematics for Golfers." In *The World of Mathematics* (vol. 4 of 4 volumes), New York: Simon & Schuster, 1956.

Mattes, J. B., "Can You Buy Spin?" *Golf* 30 (Sept. 1988).

McCallen, B., "Different Strokes." *Popular Mechanics* 165 (June 1988).

Murray, C. J. (ed.), "New Materials Take the Field: Composites Match a Golfer's Swing." *Design News* 46 (Nov. 19, 1990).

Norman, G., and P. George, *Shark Attack*. New York: Simon & Schuster, 1988.

Pelz, D., "Fine Points of Putting." *Golf* 33 (May 1991).

Sauerhaft, R., "100 Questions on Clubs, Balls, Shafts, and More." *Golf* 32 (March 1990).

Sauerhaft, R., "Out of the Lab." *Golf* 33 (April, 1991).

Walker, J., "The Amateur Scientist." *Scientific American* 240 (April 1979).

Wulf, S., "Scorecard: The Wrong One." *Sports Illustrated* 70 (June 26, 1989).

Chapter 12: Sailing

Baader, J., *The Sailing Yacht.* New York: W. W. Norton & Co., 1970.

Burr, W. M., Jr., *Sailing Tips.* New York: St. Martin's Press, 1988.

Caswell, C., "Dirt Boats." *Popular Mechanics* 165 (Jan. 1980).

Clark, N.B., "Yesterday: At the Helm of His 14-foot Catboat, Albert Einstein Was Totally at Sea." *Sports Illustrated* 63 (Oct. 21, 1985).

"Land-Yacht 'Flies' on Rigid Wing." *Design News* 46 (June 25, 1990).

Scott, D., "Wingsail Trimaran." *Popular Science* 236 (June 1990).

Chapter 13: Skiing

Diagram Group, *The Sports Fan's Ultimate Book of Sports Comparisons.* New York: St. Martin's Press, 1982.

Duda, M., "Study Links Deaths to Speed in Alpine Skiing." *The Physician and Sportsmedicine* 17 (Feb. 1989).

Frenkel, K. A., "The Leading Edge." *Forbes* 134 (Dec. 31, 1984).

Glenne, B., and J. Chalupnik, "Damping: What It Is: What It Means to You." *Skiing* 37 (Oct. 1984).

Heller, M., *The Skier's Encyclopedia.* New York: Paddington Press, 1979.

Johnson, W.O., "It's Got Its Ups and Downs: Extreme Skiing." *Sports Illustrated* 54 (March 30, 1981).

Masia, S., "Bringing in the Sheaths." *Ski Magazine* 56 (Sept. 1991).

Masia, S., "Inside and Out: What the Terms Mean." *Ski Magazine* 56 (Sept. 1991).

Murray, C. J. (ed.), "New Materials Take the Field: Better Vibration Damping for Skiers." *Design News* 46 (Nov. 19, 1990).

Perlman, E., "Anatomy of a Ski." *Science* 85 6 (Jan./Feb. 1985).

Savolainen, S., "Theoretical Drag Analysis of a Skier in the Downhill Race." *International Journal of Sport Biomechanics.* 5 (1989).

Wray, C. L., "Head-master of the Metal Ski." *Ski Magazine* 56 (Sept. 1991).

Chapter 14: Skydiving

"A Miraculous Sky Rescue." *Time* 129 (May 4, 1987).

Poynter, D., *Parachuting: The Skydiver's Handbook*. Santa Barbara, California: Para Publishing, 1989.

Sellick, B., *The Wild Wonderful World of Parachutes and Parachuting*. Englewood Cliffs, New Jersey: Prentice-Hall, 1981.

Chapter 15: Surfing

Foster, R. J., *Physical Geology*, 4th ed. Columbus, Ohio: Charles E. Merrill Publishing Co., 1983.

Hendrickson, R., *The Ocean Almanac*. New York: Doubleday & Company, 1984.

Kuhns, G. W., *On Surfing*. Bunkyo-ku, Tokyo: Charles E. Tuttle Company, 1963.

"Sharks and Surfers." *Science* 4 (Sept. 1983).

Stutz, B., "Why the Shark Bites." *Natural History* 96 (Nov. 1987).

Chapter 16: Tennis

Bernardo, S., "Physics of the Sweet Spot." *Science Digest* 92 (May 1984).

Borg, B., *My Life and Game*. New York: Simon & Schuster, 1980.

Brody, H., "Models of Tennis Racket Impacts." *International Journal of Sport Biomechanics* 3 (1987).

Brody, H., "Physics of the Tennis Racket II: The 'Sweet Spot.'" *American Journal of Physics* 49 (Sept. 1981).

Brody, H., "Vibration Damping of Tennis Rackets." *International Journal of Sport Biomechanics* 5 (1989).

Connors, J., *How to Play Tougher Tennis*. Trumbull, Connecticut: Golf Digest/Tennis, Inc., 1986.

Greenberg, J., "Traumatic Tennis: A State of Shock." *Science News* 126 (1984).

Groppel, J. L., I. Shin, J. Spots, and B. Hill, "Effects of Different String Tension Patterns and Racket Motion on Racket-Ball Impact." *International Journal of Sport Biomechanics* 3 (1987).

Lendrem, D., "Should John McEnroe Grunt?" *New Scientist* 99 (July 21, 1983).

Navratilova, M., "Switching Surfaces." *World Tennis* 34 (Oct. 1986).

Prince, S. C., "To Each His Own." *World Tennis* 37 (May 1990).

Torrey, L., *Stretching the Limits*. New York: Dodd, Mead & Co., 1985.

U. S. Professional Tennis Association, *Tennis: A Professional Guide*. New York: Kodansha International, 1984.

Widing, M.A.B., and M. Moeinzadeh, "Finite Element Modeling of a Tennis Racket With Variable String Patterns and Tensions," *International Journal of Sport Biomechanics* 6 (1990).